AutoCAD 2000
Visual JumpStart

WOK	
WOO	
LOW	2/02
MAI	
SPE	
TWY	
CON	
WAR	
MOB	
EHS	
RES	

AutoCAD® 2000
Visual JumpStart™

David Frey

SYBEX®

San Francisco ◆ Paris ◆ Düsseldorf ◆ Soest ◆ London

Associate Publisher: Cheryl Applewood
Contracts and Licensing Manager: Kristine O'Callaghan
Acquisitions & Developmental Editors: Melanie Spiller, Benjamin Tomkins
Editor: Jim Compton
Production Editor: Kylie Johnston
Technical Editor: Scott Onstott
Book Designer: Maureen Forys, Happenstance Type-O-Rama
Electronic Publishing Specialist: Maureen Forys, Happenstance Type-O-Rama
Proofreaders: Andrea Fox, Nancy Riddiough, Lindy Wolf
Indexer: Nancy Guenther
Cover Designer: Daniel Ziegler
Cover Illustrator/Photographer: Ziegler Design

Library of Congress Card Number: 00-105117

ISBN: 0-7821-2777-0

Manufactured in the United States of America

10 9 8 7 6 5 4 3 2

To John Christensen, my first AutoCAD guide—trailblazer, inspiration, vessel of humor and good will, speed demon.

Acknowledgments

The people who have helped put this book together have done an excellent job and deserve acknowledgment. I appreciate the work of Cheryl Applewood, who has served as Associate Publisher and helped a great deal at the end of the process to keep things on track, and I want to thank Maureen Forys, who designed the Visual JumpStart series and has served as Electronic Publishing Specialist for this book. She was able to create the color insert from the drawings I submitted, and make the graphics in the book work. Acquisitions and Developmental Editors Melanie Spiller and Ben Tomkins have been great. Melanie helped a great deal in the development of the original concept to make a fit between AutoCAD and the Visual Jumpstart series. Ben has been very supportive since he came on board. Jim Compton, serving as Editor, has worked very hard to keep the writing consistently clear. Thanks to Kylie Johnston, Production Editor, for keeping track of everything and monitoring the schedule. Scott Onstott has done a good job as Technical Editor. Finally, Andrea Fox, Nancy Riddiough, and Lindy Wolf have served as Proofreaders and Nancy Guenther created the index. It's a great feeling to be working with a team of people doing such a professional job.

Contents

Contents

Contents

Introduction

This book offers a fresh approach to learning AutoCAD. Designed for the beginner who may find the complexity of the program intimidating, *AutoCAD 2000 Visual JumpStart* uses a highly visual, step-by-step format to present the fundamental tasks that any new user needs in order to get "up and running" as quickly as possible on the CAD program that is the industry standard.

How This Book Is Organized

AutoCAD 2000 Visual Jumpstart can be read from the first page to the last, but each chapter is designed to be a self-contained presentation of a particular topic. So don't be afraid to jump around to find what you are looking for. When a subject refers to information in another chapter, a note will make such a reference.

The book has fifteen chapters. In Chapter 1, you'll get a tour of the AutoCAD screen, and you'll learn how to adjust the display to suit your working style and how to save drawing files. This is followed by a brief general description, in Chapter 2, of how commands are started, executed, and ended. Then, in Chapters 3 and 4, the basic commands for drawing and modifying objects are introduced and illustrated with exercises. Chapters 5–10 cover basic drawing procedures: setting up a new drawing, entering measurements and specific distances, using the object snap tools for precision, selecting lines and other objects for modifying, controlling the view of your drawing on the screen, and correcting errors. The next four chapters cover specific AutoCAD features such as layers and linetypes, text annotations, blocks (or groupings), and dimensions. Finally, Chapter 15 guides you through the process of printing your drawing.

Each chapter is organized by tasks. For each operation that you are shown how to perform—drawing straight lines or setting the units of measurement, for example—you'll see exactly what commands to enter and which options to select.

As an added bonus, there is a gallery of full-color AutoCAD drawings created by working professionals in various fields that rely on computer-assisted design, including architecture and mechanical engineering, to give you an idea of the power you are about to tap.

How to Make Good Use of This Book

I recommend using this book as a kind of beginner's reference. Use the index or table of contents to find the command or feature you want to learn about and go directly there. Each basic operation is presented as a step-by-step procedure, with illustrations to guide you. Simple but realistic examples allow you to try out most procedures on your own. As key AutoCAD terms are introduced, you'll find capsule definitions in the margin. (These definitions are also gathered into a Glossary at the end of the book, so you can look up a term at any time.) Margin notes also provide alternative methods to accomplish particular steps and summarize important concepts.

Every reader should begin with the first chapter, especially if you are not at all familiar with AutoCAD. After that, you can jump to any of the chapters that meet your needs. Keep the book near your workstation for quick access as you work on your own drawings. If a command or procedure confuses you, you can easily flip to the two or three pages that describe it.

I hope this book serves you as a useful guide in the adventure of learning AutoCAD 2000.

Part 1

Getting Going

To orient you during the process of learning the complex application AutoCAD, you'll begin this book with specific instructions for getting the program started and bringing up a new or existing drawing. Then you'll take a brief tour of the AutoCAD screen and see how you can adjust this working environment to meet your needs. In Chapter 2, you'll learn how to give instructions—commands—to the program and how commands work. Finally, in Chapters 3 and 4 you'll learn the basic commands for constructing and editing an AutoCAD drawing.

Getting Going

Chapter 1

Starting Up AutoCAD 2000

Once you have clicked the AutoCAD 2000 icon on your desktop or selected AutoCAD 2000 from the Start menu, AutoCAD begins to start up. In this chapter, I will explain how to use the Startup dialog box, take you on a quick tour of the Graphical User Interface (GUI), and show you how to save your drawing. I recommend that you read this chapter first, unless you are already familiar with the information presented here.

- The Startup dialog box

- The GUI: a quick tour and guide to settings

- Saving drawing files

Using the Startup Dialog Box

When AutoCAD starts, the Startup dialog box appears in the middle of your screen. It offers you several ways to begin your drawing session. You can open a drawing already stored on disk or you can create a new one, either entirely from scratch, based on a template, or with the help of a "wizard." The following section covers each of these options in turn.

Open an Existing Drawing

The Open a Drawing option is used for opening a drawing that has already been saved to your hard disk, a floppy disk or removable Zip disk, or a network system.

1. When the Startup dialog box opens, the button for the method you (or another user) *last* used to start AutoCAD is selected (in this case, Start from Scratch). Instead, click the Open a Drawing button.

ToolTip

The small text box that appears on the screen to help you identify toolbar and dialog box buttons.

Tip

When you hold the cursor on a button without clicking, a **ToolTip** appears that identifies the button.

2. The middle of the dialog box now displays a list of drawings that have been opened recently. Highlight one of the names in the list to see a preview image of that drawing.

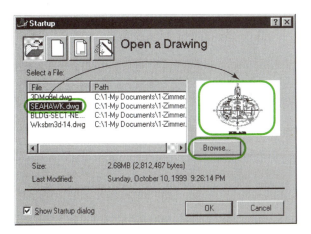

3. If the drawing you want is not in the list, click the Browse button to choose a drawing from the Sample folder, or navigate to another one that has been made available on your file system by another user.

4. In the Select File dialog box, navigate your way to the correct folder and open it. Then, find your drawing in the list and highlight it. A preview image of that drawing is displayed.

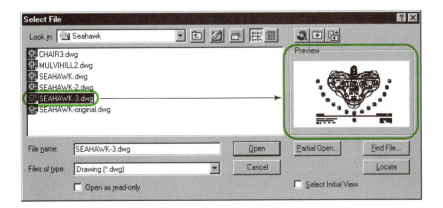

5. Click the Open button.

6. Your drawing will be opened in AutoCAD, ready to work on.

AutoCAD drawing files use the .dwg extension.

If the drawing you want is in the list of recently opened drawings, highlight it and click OK to bring it up.

The Select File dialog box operates like similar dialog boxes in other Windows-compatible applications.

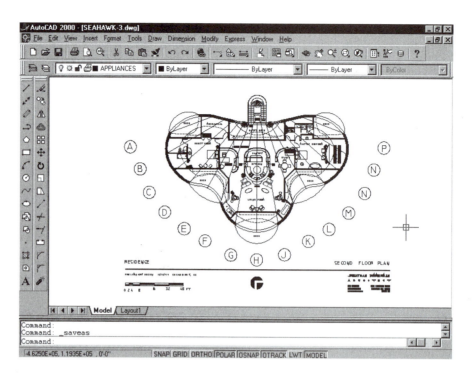

Start a New Drawing from Scratch

Default setting

The preset value that will be used unless a setting has been changed (customized).

The Start from Scratch option creates a blank drawing using AutoCAD's **default settings**, similar to the blank sheet when starting a new file with a word-processing application. If you just want to start drawing but aren't sure how big a sheet you will need yet, use this option. You can be more specific about the size later.

1. On the Startup screen, ignore whatever startup method was selected previously (Open a Drawing in the example below) and select the Start from Scratch button.

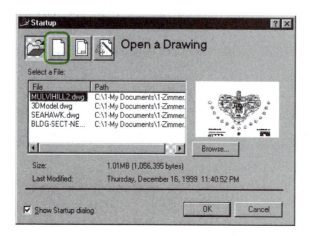

2. In the Default Settings area, you can choose between English and Metric measurements. Click the OK button. AutoCAD will bring up a blank drawing.

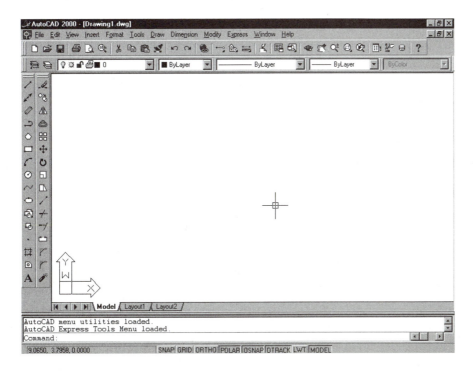

We will take a tour of the screen in the next section.

Tip

If you click the Cancel button in the Startup dialog box, AutoCAD will always start up as if you had clicked the Start from Scratch button, regardless of which of the four upper buttons is depressed in the dialog box.

Use a Template to Start a New Drawing

If you want to use a pre-drawn border and title block at a specific sheet size for your new drawing, use the Template option.

Template drawing
A drawing used as a pattern for new drawings.

Tip

You can create your own **template drawing** and include it in the list of templates that come with AutoCAD. This is great if you find yourself using the same borders or text all the time.

1. On the Startup screen, ignore whatever startup method was selected previously (Start from Scratch in the example below) and click the Template option.

2. Scroll down the list of template files and highlight one that you are interested in. An image preview of that template will be displayed.

Most template files are kept in the AutoCAD 2000\ Template folder, but if you know of additional locations where they might be stored, use the Browse button to navigate to a different folder.

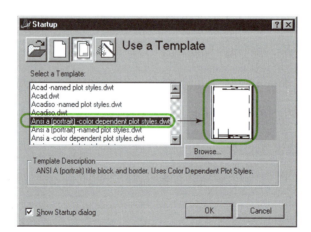

3. Click OK. A new drawing comes up based on the chosen template.

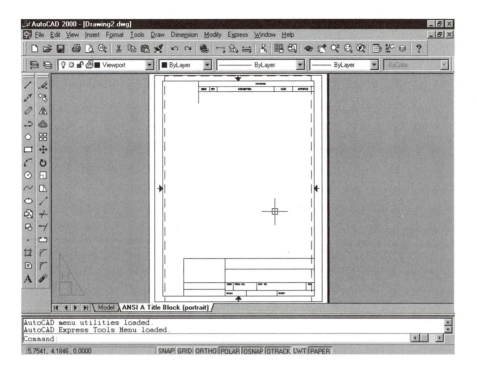

Use a Wizard to Start a New Drawing

There are two **wizards** to help you set up parameters for a new drawing: Quick, which has two criteria, and Advanced, with five. Let's work through the steps of the Quick Setup Wizard.

1. On the Startup screen, ignore whatever startup method was selected previously (Use a Template in the example below) and instead click the Use a Wizard button.

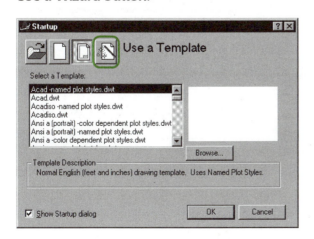

Wizard
Short routines that lead you through a series of steps to accomplish a task.

9

2. Highlight Quick Setup and click OK.

Unit of measurement

The kind of quantity used for a distance, such as inch, foot, mile, meter, etc.

Decimal units can represent any length. 12 decimal units could be 12 inches, 12 yards, 12 miles, 12 meters, etc. Architectural units are specifically feet and inches.

3. Click on a **unit of measurement**, and then click Next. For this example, I used decimal units.

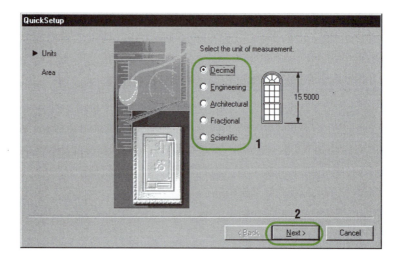

4. Enter a Width and Length for your drawing sheet. I used 12 for the width and 9 for the length. Then click Finish.

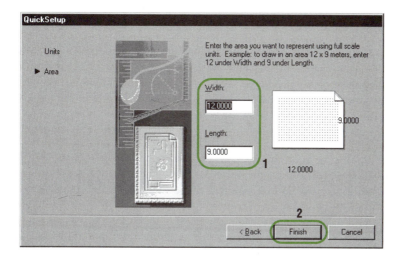

5. A new drawing comes up. It has the Units and Area that you set with the wizard.

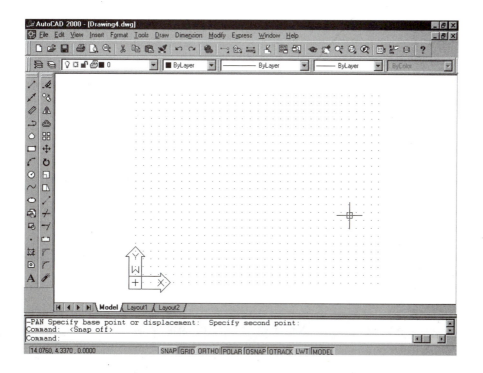

Note

Once AutoCAD is running, you can access the Startup dialog box by clicking File ➤ New on the pull-down menus. It's the same dialog box you got when you started up AutoCAD, except that the Open a Drawing button is not available.

How the Screen Is Organized— a Quick Tour and Setup Guide

Graphical User Interface (GUI)

The way the monitor screen looks when AutoCAD is running, with its various parts, like toolbars, menus, the drawing area, and so on.

This section will take you on a quick tour of the **Graphical User Interface** (GUI) and show you how to set up each component to match the monitor screens shown in this book. The changes you will be shown how to make are some of the most basic types of customization that are possible. It's purely optional to make these setting changes, but you should at least take the tour if you're not familiar with AutoCAD.

Tip

You may want to keep your setup as it is for a variety of reasons. AutoCAD offers a tool called Profiles for saving and restoring several screen setup configurations. See *Mastering AutoCAD 2000*, by George Omura (Sybex, 1999), for details.

Locating the Title Bar and Pull-Down Menus

Pull-down menu

A set of commands displayed when the menu name is clicked.

At the top of the screen, AutoCAD displays a title bar and a menu bar with **pull-down menus**. The title bar displays the name of the application and the name of the current drawing at the left end, and the three window control buttons for AutoCAD at the right end.

Menu bar   Window control buttons

Title bar

Below the title bar, you'll find the Menu bar. It contains the pull-down menus. Some of these menus contain only AutoCAD commands, and others are used in most Windows applications but have some AutoCAD commands on them. We'll start with an AutoCAD-specific menu, Draw.

1. Click the Draw menu.

2. On the Draw menu, choose Point. A **cascading menu** appears.

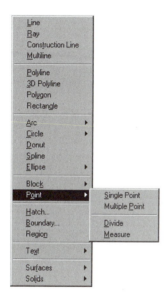

Cascading menu
A sub-menu that flies out from a pull-down menu when an item on it is clicked.

A small arrow to the right of a menu item indicates that clicking the item will display a cascading menu with further options.

3. Press the Esc key twice to remove the menus or click on a blank part of the screen that's outside the drawing area.

  Tip

When you have a menu pulled down, if you click on the drawing area, a selection window begins. If you click on a **toolbar**, a command begins. If you click on the command window, the cursor becomes a text cursor. You must click on a blank area of the screen to remove the menus without making something else happen.

Toolbar
A grouping of icons, or small pictures, that represent related commands.

Bringing Up Toolbars and Docking Them

You probably have some toolbars already on your screen. Deciding which toolbars to display—that is, which tools you want to have at your fingertips—is an essential part of customizing your workspace. To give you some practice, let's

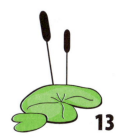

bring other toolbars onto the screen and dock them. Then you will remove them to see what that's like.

1. The toolbar that is just under the Menu bar is the Standard toolbar. Move the cursor onto the toolbar and place it on one of the icons. They become buttons and a ToolTip appears, identifying the command.

2. Right-click any of the buttons. A menu appears with a list of available toolbars.

On the Toolbar menu, those toolbars currently visible on the screen have a checkmark next to them.

Docked toolbar
A toolbar whose location has been temporarily fixed outside the drawing area, but near its edge.

3. Click on Inquiry on the Toolbar menu. The Inquiry toolbar appears. It has commands that help you get information about your drawing.

4. Click on the title bar of the toolbar, hold down the mouse button, and drag it to the right side of the drawing area.

5. When the rectangle changes its shape, release the mouse button. The toolbar will be **docked** on the right side of the screen.

6. Move the cursor to the double bars at the top of the docked Inquiry toolbar, hold down the left mouse button, and drag the toolbar onto the screen.

7. Release the mouse button. The toolbar regains its title bar.

> Toolbars on the drawing area have title bars and are called "floating toolbars."

8. Click the toolbar's Close button.

The toolbar is removed from the screen.

The Drawing Area—Setting the Background Color

The large open area in the middle of the screen where you construct your drawing is called the **drawing area**. You can control its background color using the Options dialog box.

1. Open the Options dialog box from the Tools menu.

Drawing area
The large, blank portion of the AutoCAD screen where you create your drawing.

15

2. In the Options dialog box, click the Display tab.

The best background color for the drawing area depends on the lighting in your room and the colors you use for the lines in your drawing. A black background works well in a brightly lit room and highlights the brighter colors like green and yellow. The white background color does just the opposite.

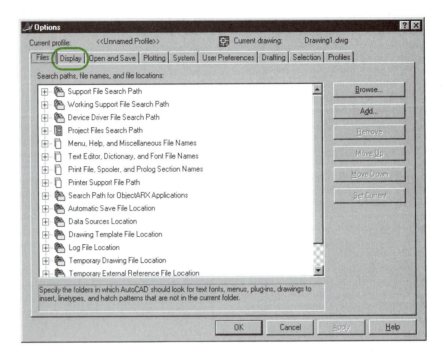

3. On the Display tab, click the Colors button.

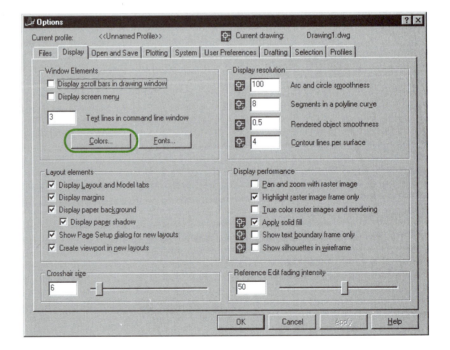

4. In the Color Options dialog box, check the Window Element drop-down list to be sure Model Tab Background is displayed. If it's not, open the list and choose it.

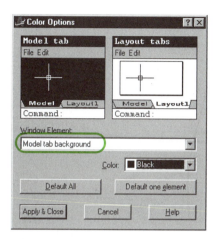

5. Open the Color drop-down list, and choose White.

6. Click the Apply & Close button.

7. In the Options dialog box, click OK.

Scrollbars—How to Turn Them Off

The **scrollbars** on the right and bottom of the drawing area aren't necessary because there are AutoCAD tools that do the same thing in a better way. These scrollbars also take up space that could be used for the drawing area. Of course, if you are comfortable with them and prefer to use them, leave them on the screen.

1. Open the Options dialog box from the Tools menu.

2. In the Options dialog box, click the Display tab.

Scrollbar

A strip with arrow buttons and a slider on the side of the drawing. It is used for sliding the current drawing around on the screen.

17

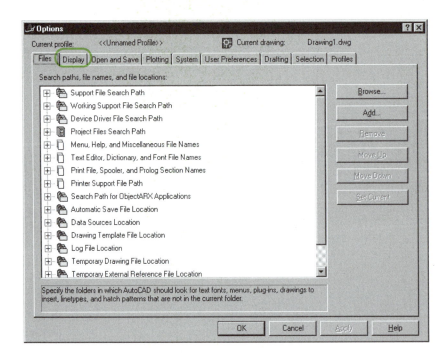

3. On the Display tab, uncheck the Display Scroll Bars in Drawing Window check box.

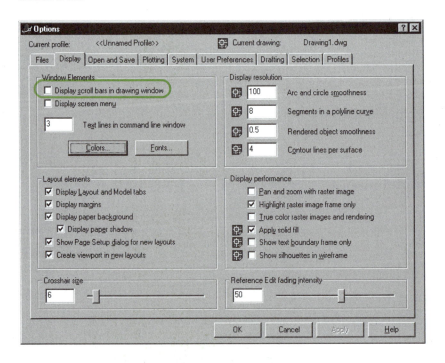

4. Click Apply, and click OK.

See Also Chapter 9 covers techniques for controlling the view of your drawing.

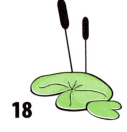

The Command Window—Setting the Number of Lines of Text

The Command window is where AutoCAD gives you instructions and feedback as it executes commands for you. It is helpful to have at least three lines of text displayed here.

> Some commands present information on all three lines of text in the command window.

1. Check your Command window for the number of lines of text displayed. If you already have three lines, go on to the next section.

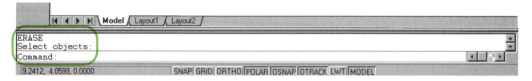

2. To change the number of lines, click Tools ➢ Options to open the Options dialog box.

3. In the Options dialog box, click the Display tab.

4. On the Display tab, check the Text Lines in Command Line Window text box. Change this number to 3.

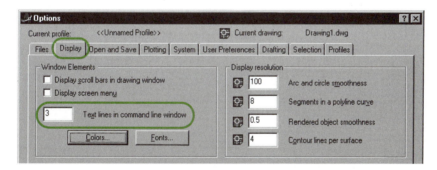

> You can have more than three lines of text, but this takes up space that could be used by the drawing area.

5. Click Apply, and then Click OK.

The Status Bar—Setting the Buttons to On or Off

At the very bottom of the screen, you'll see a coordinate display and a set of buttons.

> ***x, y, z* coordinate**
> Three numbers, separated by commas, that specify the location of a point in 3D space.

1. Move the crosshair on the screen and keep your eye on the coordinate display. It displays the position of the crosshair in an *x, y, z* **coordinate**.

19

See Also   You will learn more about the coordinate display in Chapter 6: "Working with Distances and Directions."

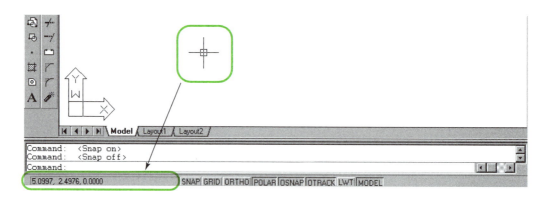

2. Click the Snap button until it looks pressed ("in"). This is the On position. When the button is in the "out" position, it is Off.

3. Click any buttons on the status bar necessary to make the Model button on the far right set to On and the rest of the buttons set to Off.

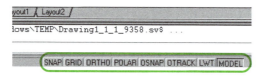

Most of the functions of these buttons will be explained later in the book.

The UCS Icon—Turning It Off

The icon in the lower left of the drawing area is called the User Coordinate System icon, or UCS icon.

The orientation of the UCS tells you the current directions of the *x and y axes*. You won't need to know too much about this feature for this book, but let's look at it so you'll know how to hide it if you prefer.

1. Open the View pull-down menu.

2. Click Display, and then click UCS Icon.

3. Click On to remove the checkmark and turn off the UCS icon.

The Crosshair—Setting Its Size

The **crosshair cursor** is the form of the cursor that AutoCAD uses for drawing lines. For clarity in this book, I will set the lines of the crosshair to be short. You may want them to extend to the edges of the drawing area on your own screen.

1. Click Tools ➢ Options to open the Options dialog box.

2. In the Options dialog box, click the Display tab.

3. On the Display tab, drag the sliding handle for the Crosshair Size to the right or left. The text box will read the percentage of the screen that the crosshairs will extend across. For the book, the size is set to 6%.

x and y axes
The two directions—left/right and up/down—that define the plane used to draw on in AutoCAD.

Crosshair cursor
A form of the cursor that consists of intersecting vertical and horizontal lines. Their intersection is the current location of the cursor.

By setting the crosshair to be long, you have the advantage of being able to line things up vertically and horizontally on the screen.

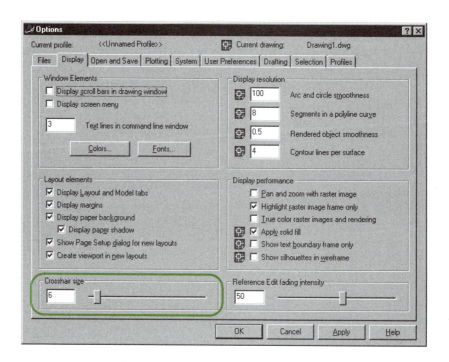

4. Click Apply and then OK.

This completes the tour of the AutoCAD graphical user interface. If you followed the steps, the various elements on your screen should be set up to follow the book, or to your preference.

Saving Drawing Files

When you end a drawing session, there are several ways you can save your work. These options are illustrated below.

Saving a New Drawing File

When you finish working on a new drawing that has not been saved yet, the drawing will need to be named and stored in a folder.

1. Click the Save button on the Standard toolbar.

2. In the Save Drawing As dialog box, navigate to the folder where you want to save the new drawing. Open that folder.

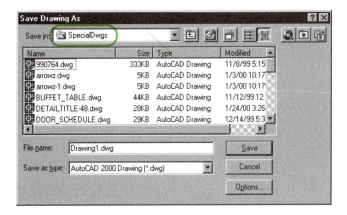

3. In the File Name text box, type in the drawing's name.

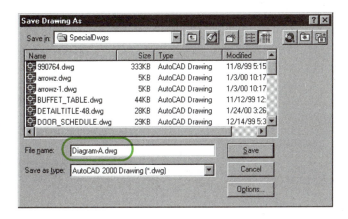

4. Click the Save button.

When naming an AutoCAD drawing, you don't need to enter the file extension name (.dwg). AutoCAD does this automatically.

23

5. Back in the main AutoCAD window, check the title bar to be sure it includes the new name of the drawing.

Saving an Existing Drawing File

When you finish working on an existing drawing that has already been named and located in a folder, all you need to do to save your changes is to click the Save button.

It is wise to periodically save an existing drawing as you are working on it.

Giving an Existing Drawing File a New Name

If you have changed an existing drawing and want to save it separately from the original drawing, save it with a new name. You might do this if you are creating a second version of the same original drawing.

1. Open the File pull-down menu and click Save As.

2. In the Save Drawing As dialog box, navigate to the folder that will contain the new drawing. Open that folder.

3. In the File Name text box, type in the drawing's new name.

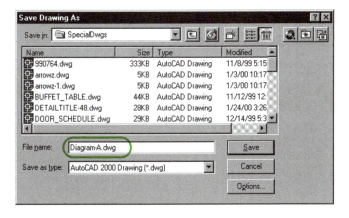

4. Click the Save button in the dialog box.

5. Check the Title Bar to be sure it includes the new name of the drawing.

You'll find that the old version of the drawing still exists in its unsaved version with the original name, and you have a new second drawing with the saved changes and the new name.

What's Next?

This chapter introduced you to the AutoCAD GUI. It also illustrated how to start up AutoCAD, adjust some of the default settings of the GUI, and save drawing files in various ways. The next chapter is an overview of the procedures for executing commands in AutoCAD.

Chapter 2

Understanding How Commands Work

In AutoCAD there are a large number of commands at your disposal. You will learn the basic commands in this book and, over time, get familiar with others. This chapter is meant to be used as a reference, to help you get a general idea of how commands work. After reading Chapter 1, you can choose to skip this chapter and move on to Chapters 3 and 4, to learn a few of the basic commands, before returning to this chapter for an overview.

- Starting commands
- Executing commands
- Ending commands

Starting Commands

Each **command** discussed in this book can be started in several ways. We will mostly be using toolbars and pull-down menus to start commands, but in this chapter we will also look at how commands are initiated and executed from the keyboard.

Using Toolbar Icon Buttons to Start Commands

The toolbars have icons for the most-used commands. An icon changes into a button when you roll the pointer cursor over it, and you can then click it to start the command. Using the toolbars is often the quickest way to start commands, so you should note whether the command you want is on a toolbar that is currently on the screen.

1. Move the cursor to the toolbar that contains the icon of the command you wish to start, and hold the **pointer arrow** on the icon until a *ToolTip* appears. It identifies the icon. At the same time, the icon now seems to be on a button.

2. Click and release the left mouse button while keeping the pointer on the button.

When the command starts:

3. A dialog box may appear on the screen, depending on the command you choose.

> Dialog boxes usually contain several options for completing a command.

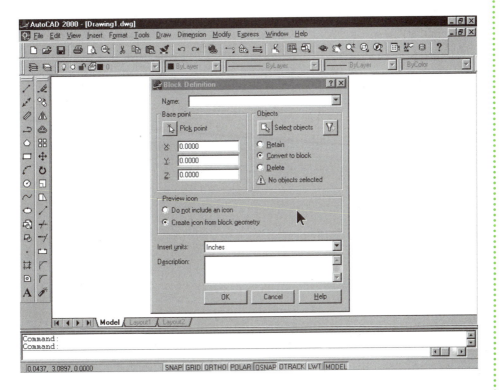

Or:

4. The Command window may change and **prompt** you to take the next step in the command.

> **Prompt**
> The information or choices on the Command line that AutoCAD requests from you.

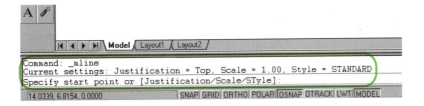

Starting a Command from a Toolbar Flyout

Some command buttons are on **toolbar flyouts**. The flyout can be opened to allow you access to all the command buttons on the flyout.

1. Move the pointer cursor to any button that has a flyout. These buttons have a black arrow below and to the right of the button icon.

Some of the toolbar flyouts can be opened and docked like regular toolbars.

2. Place the pointer arrow on the button and hold down the left mouse button. The flyout will open.

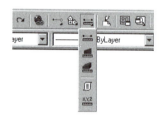

Once a command from a flyout is used, its button replaces the flyout button that was on the original toolbar. You can then just click on the top flyout button to execute that command without having to reopen the flyout.

3. Keep holding down the left mouse button and move the pointer cursor down the flyout. Stop it on the button you think you want. A ToolTip will identify the button.

4. Release the button, and the command begins.

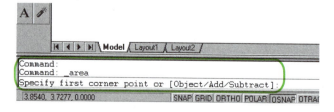

Using Pull-Down Menus to Start Commands

The pull-down menus contain most of the commands you will need to use in AutoCAD.

1. Move the cursor to the pull-down menu bar and rest the pointer on the menu title that you want to open. The selected menu title will look like it's on a button. Click on the menu. The menu opens.

2. Move the pointer down the menu to the command you wish to start.

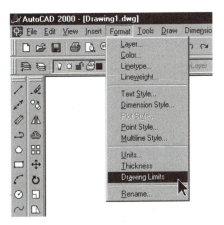

3. Click on the menu item. The menu disappears and the command begins.

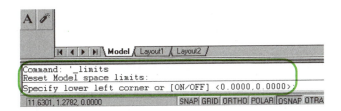

Using the Keyboard to Start Commands

Many users consider the keyboard the fastest way to start and run commands.

1. Look at the Command window and be sure the Command **prompt** is on the bottom line. If not, press the Esc key until Command: appears there.

Almost all of the commands on the toolbars can be found on the pull-down menus.

Commands on the pull-down menus that have an ellipsis (. . .) are executed using dialog boxes. The others use the command line. If you need a refresher, see Chapter 1.

In this chapter and throughout the book, "click" means to click and release the left mouse button. When you need to click the right mouse button, I will say "right-click."

Command prompt
Text that says **Command:** on the bottom line of the Command window. It tells you that no commands are currently running, and it's waiting for you to enter the next command.

31

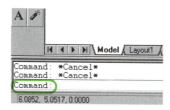

2. Type in the name of the command.

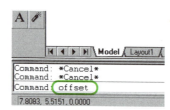

3. Press ↵. The command begins.

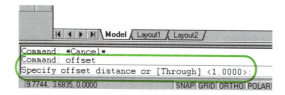

With so many available ways to start commands, you will need to find the method, or combination of methods, that best serves you.

Executing Commands

Once a command has been started, several actions may be required to complete the execution of the command. As you finish one stage of the command and begin the next, the Command window will prompt you for what you need to do next, and the cursor will often change its form.

Working with the Command Prompt

The lines in the Command window give you the information you need to execute a command. They are as follows:

1. The display of the Command prompt (Command:) on the bottom line of the Command window is AutoCAD's signal to you that no commands are running. This means that you can now start a command.

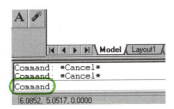

2. Once a command is started, the command's name is usually—but not always—displayed on one of the three command lines. The bottom line prompts you to take an action.

See Also   You can use the Options dialog box to set the number of lines displayed in the Command window. See Chapter 1 for instructions.

3. Sometimes the bottom line prompts you to make choices.

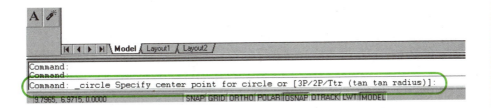

You may have to enter data, click buttons in a dialog box, pick points on the screen, or all three, in the course of a command.

In the Command window, the command that's been started usually has an underscore (_) before its name.

You can choose a command option by entering its capitalized letters.

33

4. Sometimes the bottom line prompts you to enter data:

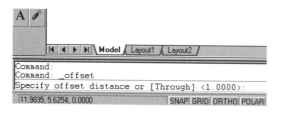

5. When a command has finished executing, you'll see Command: again on the bottom line.

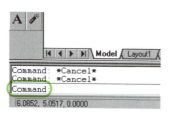

How the Cursor Changes in the Course of a Command

The AutoCAD cursor may take on several forms in the course of a command being executed. Each form gives you a clue about what you need to do at the time.

1. When no command is running, the cursor has a **pickbox** superimposed on the crosshair.

See Also You can adjust the length of the crosshairs. See Chapter 1.

2. When you are prompted to select items on the screen, the pickbox appears by itself.

☐

3. The crosshair by itself indicates that you need to pick reference points in the drawing.

4. When you move the cursor (in any of its forms) off the drawing area, it changes to the standard selection pointer.

The cursor will also change to a pointer when it moves onto a dialog box, menu, or toolbar that is on the drawing area.

Ending Commands

Some commands automatically end when they have done their work. Others will continue to be active until you end them yourself. For example, the Circle command ends once one circle is drawn. On the other hand, the Line command stays running until you end it, because it assumes you will want to draw multiple line segments that are connected to each other. You must tell AutoCAD to end the Line command. There are three tools to end commands.

When a command ends, **Command:** is displayed in the bottom line of text in the Command window.

Using the Enter Key to End a Command

Pressing the Enter key will do different things at different times in the execution of a command. It is particularly useful for ending commands.

1. When you have finished using a command, but it hasn't ended, a prompt for further action will still be on the bottom line of the Command window.

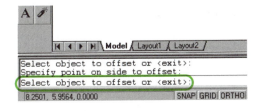

2. Press the Enter key. The command ends, and the Command: prompt returns.

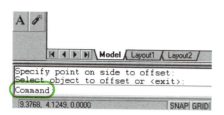

Right-Clicking to End a Command

Right-clicking the mouse performs several functions, including that of ending a command.

1. When you have finished using a command, but it hasn't ended, a prompt for further action will still be on the bottom line of the Command window.

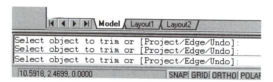

The shortcut menu offers several options for the current command.

2. Right-click. The shortcut menu appears on the screen near the cursor.

You can set the right-click function to do exactly what pressing ↵ does. Go to Tools ➤ Options, open the User Preferences tab, and click the Right-Click Customization button. Then change the settings to your preference.

3. Click Enter on the shortcut menu. The command ends and the Command prompt returns.

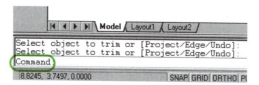

See Also Pressing the Esc key once or twice will cancel a command at any point in the course of its execution. See Chapter 10: "Correcting Errors."

Tip

You can restart the command that just ended by pressing ↵, or by right-clicking, then clicking the top item on the shortcut menu.

Summary

This chapter has been a general summary of the basic features of how commands work in AutoCAD. I hope it will make learning the commands less of an ordeal and more of an adventure for you.

Chapter 3

Drawing

Use the Draw commands to create new lines and other items in your drawing. We'll look at several of the most basic Draw commands, all of which are on the Draw toolbar on the left side of the screen. Commands you will learn can be divided into four groups:

- Straight lines
- Arcs
- Closed shapes
- Special lines

Drawing Straight Lines

The Line command enables you to draw a single straight line or a series of straight-line segments that are connected end-to-end in order to make shapes with several sides.

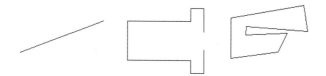

Drawing a Single Straight Line

To draw a line, you need to pick two points. These points will become the endpoints of the line.

The Line command can also be found on the Draw menu, and can be started by typing **l ↵** on the keyboard. (That's an L, not a 1.)

1. Pick the Line icon on the Draw toolbar to start the Line command.

When I say to "pick a point" I mean to click the left mouse button when the cursor is at a desired point in the drawing area.

2. Pick a point where you want to start the line. Then move the crosshair cursor away from the point you picked. Notice the **rubber-banding** effect of the line that connects the cursor with the point you just picked.

Rubber banding

The appearance of a line stretching from the last point picked to the crosshair.

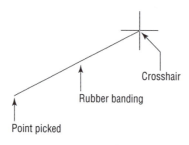

Crosshair

Rubber banding

Point picked

3. Pick a second point and move the crosshair away from that point. The rubber-banding line is the beginning of the second line segment, but in this case you want only one segment.

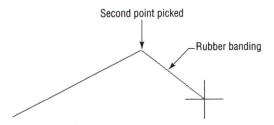

Second point picked

Rubber banding

4. Right-click the mouse. This will bring up a **shortcut menu** next to the crosshair.

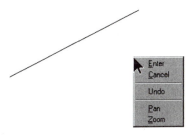

Enter
Cancel

Undo

Pan
Zoom

Shortcut menu

A small menu that appears on the screen near the cursor when you right-click the mouse. It is context-sensitive; i.e., its commands will change according to what you're doing at the moment. It is also called a Context menu.

5. Choose Enter from the shortcut menu. The line is finished and the Line command has ended.

Drawing Several Connected Line Segments

If you are drawing a box or the layout of a room, you will use the Line command to make several connected line segments.

1. Start the Line command again.

2. Pick two points to draw the first line, just as you did in the previous section in steps 2 and 3.

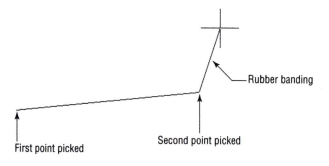

3. Pick a third point to draw the second segment.

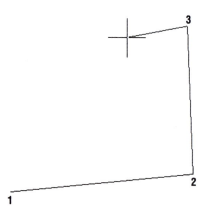

4. Continue to pick points until you have picked the eighth point.

You can press ↵, or right-click and click Enter on the shortcut menu, at any time to end the Line command. The segments you have drawn so far will remain.

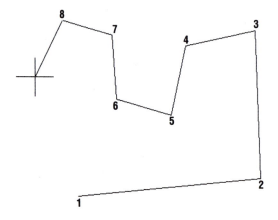

5. Right-click and pick Close on the shortcut menu to **close** the shape.

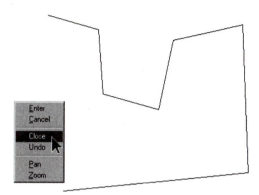

Close
An option of the Line command that instructs AutoCAD to draw a line from the second point of the final line segment to the start point of the first segment, thereby closing the shape.

AutoCAD draws a line from point 8 to point 1, closing the shape, and the Line command automatically ends.

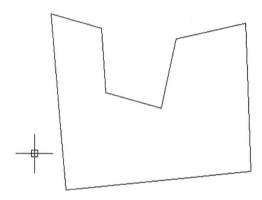

See Also   To control the exact length of any line and to make a line exactly vertical or horizontal, see Chapter 6: "Working with Distances and Directions."

Drawing Arcs

Although the arc is a simple geometric shape, there are so many options for drawing an arc that it can all be a little confusing at first. By clicking Arc on the Draw pull-down menu, you can see the options on a cascading menu.

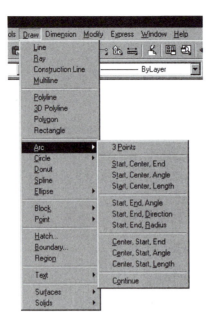

Each option displays a short summary of the input necessary to create an arc. We'll go over three of the options here and you'll get the idea. Then you can experiment with the rest.

The 3 Points Arc Option

The 3 Points option is just what it says. You pick any three points on the screen. The first one is the start point of the arc. The second is a point somewhere on the arc. Finally, the third point becomes the endpoint of the arc.

The 3 Points option is used when you know the first and last points of an arc and a third point that the arc goes through.

1. Open the Draw pull-down menu and pick Arc.

2. Click the 3 Points option on the cascading Arc menu.

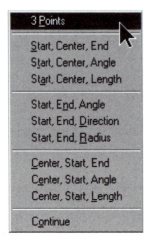

3. Pick the first point, and then move the crosshair away from that point. A rubber-banding line will dynamically stretch from the point last picked to the crosshair.

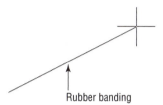

Rubber banding

3. Pick the second point, and then move the cursor around to see the possible arcs you can draw. The end of the arc moves with the crosshair.

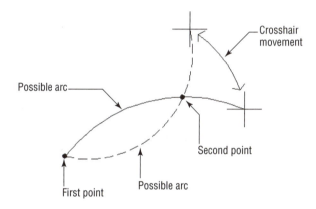

Crosshair movement

Possible arc

Second point

Possible arc

First point

4. Pick the third point to finish the arc. The Arc command will end automatically.

With this Arc option, you can make the arc curve in either direction.

The Start, Center, End Arc Option

With the Start, Center, End option, AutoCAD assumes that you are drawing an arc that curves in a counterclockwise direction, away from the first point picked, and around a center point.

1. From the cascading Arc menu on the Draw menu, pick Start, Center, End.

In AutoCAD, angles are measured positively in a counterclockwise direction, and negatively in the clockwise direction.

2. Pick a point to start the arc; then move the crosshair away from that point. A rubber-banding line will dynamically stretch from the point picked to the crosshair.

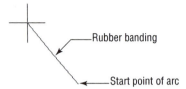

The center of an arc is like the center of a circle, not the midpoint of a curve.

3. Pick a point to serve as the center of the arc—not the midpoint of the curve—but the point around which the arc will curve.

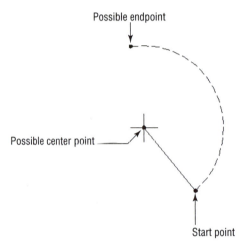

Ortho

A mode that forces lines to be drawn horizontally or vertically.

4. Move the crosshair back to a point near the first point picked. Then gradually move the crosshair in a counterclockwise direction around the center point. Make sure **Ortho** is off.

See Also Chapter 6: "Working with Distances and Directions" discusses the use of Ortho mode.

The arc will appear and change length as the cursor moves around the center point.

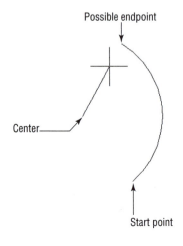

5. When the arc is the length that you want, click to establish the end-point of the arc. AutoCAD will complete the arc, and the Arc command will end.

In AutoCAD, an arc is a portion of a circle.

The Start, End, Radius Arc Option

This option of the Arc command requires that you first pick the start point and the endpoint of the arc. Then you specify the **radius** of the curve, either by typing a value or by dragging a rubber-banding line. Use this Arc option when you need an arc with a specific radius to span between two points.

Radius
The distance from the center point of an arc or circle to the arc or circle.

1. From the cascading Arc menu on the Draw menu, pick Start, End, Radius.

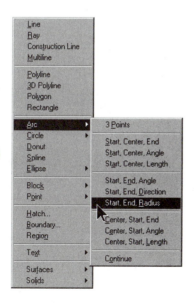

2. Pick a point to start the arc, and then move the crosshair away from that point. A rubber-banding line will stretch from the point just picked to the crosshair.

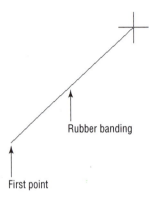

Rubber banding

First point

3. When the crosshair is where you want the arc to end, click.

4. At this point, you have two alternatives: in the Command window, type in the radius that you want and press ↵; or move the crosshairs to create a rubber-banding line and click. The length of the rubber-band line becomes the radius value. Either method completes the arc and ends the Arc command.

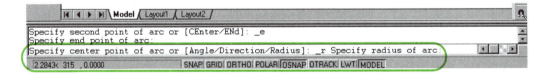

Note

Picking a point to establish the radius length is usually impractical.

Each option for drawing arcs requires a slightly different set of information about the arc. Depending on what information you have, you can choose the appropriate Arc option.

Drawing Closed Shapes

The four commands you'll explore in this section—Circle, Ellipse, Rectangle, and Polygon—are all for drawing simple closed shapes. Each one operates a little differently from the others.

Making Circles

Circles can be drawn in AutoCAD in six ways. Let's look at the first option, specifying the circle's center and radius.

1. On the Draw pull-down menu, pick Circle. The Circle cascading menu appears, displaying the six options for drawing a circle.

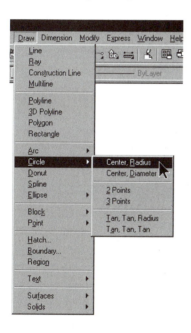

2. Pick the Center, Radius option.

AutoCAD users find that it is often easier to draw complete circles and then trim them to make arcs, than using the Arc command options. See the Circle command next in this chapter.

49

3. Pick a point in the drawing to represent the center of the circle. Then move the crosshair away from that point. A circle appears.

The rubber-banding line acts as the radius of the circle.

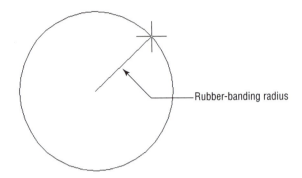

Rubber-banding radius

4. In the Command window, type in the radius for the circle and press ↵.

You can also pick a point to set the radius instead of entering a distance on the keyboard.

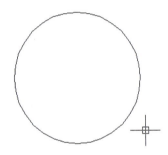

Tip

The Center, Diameter option works the same way as the Center, Radius option, except that the number you enter serves as a diameter rather than a radius. Another handy option for constructing a circle is the 2 Points option. In this one, you pick any two points, and they define the diameter of the circle.

Axis
A line about which a figure is symmetrical.

Drawing Ellipses

Ellipses have two perpendicular **axes** and are drawn by determining the length and location of each axis.

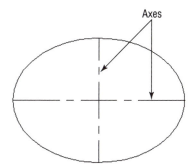

Axes

1. Pick the Ellipse icon from the Draw toolbar.

2. Pick a point to locate the endpoint of one axis; then move the cursor away from that point.

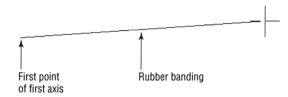

First point
of first axis

Rubber banding

One axis of an ellipse is always longer than the other one.

3. Pick a second point to be the other endpoint of the first axis. A figure that looks like a circle with a radius line will appear.

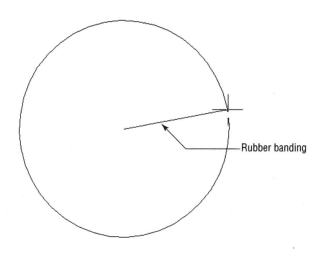

Rubber banding

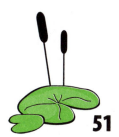

51

The rubber-banding line that stretches from the center of the ellipse to the crosshair represents half the length of the second axis.

4. Move the cursor closer and then farther from the center of the circle. The radius line rubber-bands, and the figure will change to an ellipse as you move the mouse.

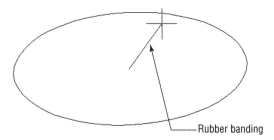

Rubber banding

5. When the ellipse is the shape you want it, click once to complete it. The Ellipse command will end.

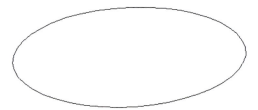

Note

The three points you picked determined the full length of the first axis and half the length of the second axis. There is also a Center option in which you determine first the center of the ellipse, and then half the lengths of the two axes.

See Also To learn how to control the exact lengths of the axes and to make them exactly vertical or horizontal, see Chapter 6.

Tip

The Ellipse command can also be found on the Draw pull-down menu, and you can launch it by typing **el** ↵ on the keyboard. (That's EL, upper or lowercase.)

Constructing Rectangles

AutoCAD has a special tool for constructing rectangles that are made with horizontal and vertical sides. To construct one, you pick two points that will become two opposite corners of the rectangle.

1. Pick the Rectangle icon on the Draw toolbar.

You can also launch the Rectangle command by picking Rectangle from the Draw pull-down menu, or by typing **rect** ↵.

2. Pick a point for the lower-left corner of the rectangle. Then move the cursor away from that point. A rectangle begins to form.

 Tip

When the lines of the crosshair cursor line up with the lines of the rectangle, both disappear. So the upper-right corner of the rectangle looks a little strange at this point in the process.

3. For the width and height of the rectangle, type **@*width,height*** ↵. For example, for a rectangle with a width of 4 and a height of 3, you would type **@4,3** ↵. This completes the rectangle and ends the Rectangle command.

You can also complete the rectangle by picking a point on the screen, instead of entering distances.

See Also The @ symbol (Shift+2) tells AutoCAD that the numbers following it are distances from the first point picked. For more information on this, see Chapter 6, "Working with Distances and Directions."

See Also Rectangles are made up of special lines called polylines, which are covered later in this chapter.

Drawing Polygons

AutoCAD's Polygon command is used for drawing a **regular polygon** with any number of sides. First you tell AutoCAD the number of sides the polygon will have. Then you specify the location of the polygon's center and determine its size.

Regular polygon

Any closed shape made up of three or more straight sides of equal length. Triangles, squares, pentagons, hexagons, and octagons are all regular polygons.

1. Pick the Polygon icon on the Draw toolbar.

The number of sides you enter must be at least 3 and no more than 1024, but specifying any more than 9 sides results in a polygon that begins to look like a circle.

2. At the Command prompt, type the number of sides you wish and press ↵.

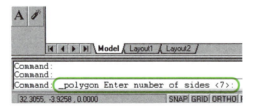

3. When prompted to Specify center of polygon or [Edge]:, pick a point for the center of the new polygon. A new prompt is displayed in the Command window:

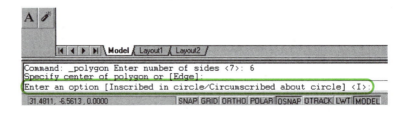

4. This prompt is a bit confusing at first. It refers to the imaginary circle that will be defined by the radius you'll specify in the next step. If you choose the default Inscribed in Circle option, the radius extends to the intersection of two sides of the polygon. If you choose Circumscribed, it extends to the midpoint of a side. Press ↵ to accept the default. The polygon is displayed. It changes size and rotates with any movement of the crosshair.

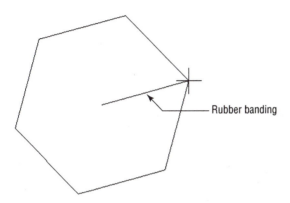

Rubber banding

5. In the Command window, type in a distance for the radius of the polygon and press ↵. The polygon is completed and the command ends.

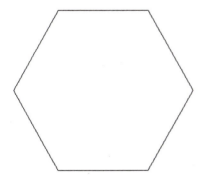

Tip

When you type in a distance, AutoCAD orients the polygon so that one side is horizontal and on the bottom. You can also pick a point to determine the radius and rotation of the polygon, instead of typing in a distance.

Note

There is also an Edge option for drawing polygons. This allows you to determine the size of the polygon by specifying the length of one of the sides.

See Also   Polygons, like rectangles, are made up of polylines. See the next section for more details.

Using Special Lines

In AutoCAD, there are several kinds of lines that have unique properties and can be used for special purposes. Two of the most important are polylines and splines.

Polylines—a Tour

Polylines—or plines for short—are drawn just like regular lines, but a series of pline segments behave as if they were one line. That is, if you select one segment of a pline, all segments are selected. Here is a quick tour of some of the pline's characteristics.

1. Choose the Polyline icon on the Draw toolbar.

You can also launch the Polyline command by clicking Polyline on the Draw pulldown menu, or by typing **pl** ↵. (This is a lowercase PL, not p1.)

2. Draw a series of line segments just like you did with the Line command.

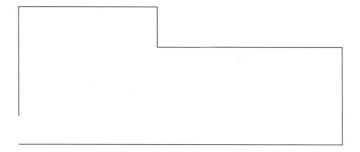

That's it—you've created a basic polyline. Now let's look at a few variations. Some of the segments can be arcs:

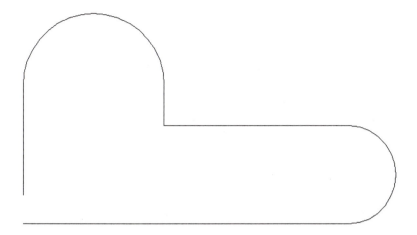

Polylines can have width (thickness).

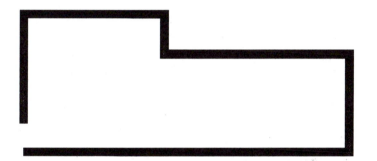

The width of a polyline can be set before the line is drawn, or afterward.

You can round all of the pline's corners to the same radius in one step:

See Also   To round corners, use the Fillet command. See Chapter 4: "Making Changes" for more on this command.

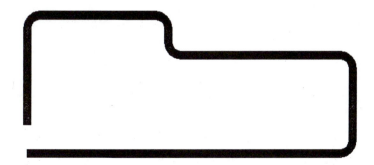

You can also smooth the edges into curves:

Smoothed polylines can be either a series of arcs or a series of very short straight-line segments.

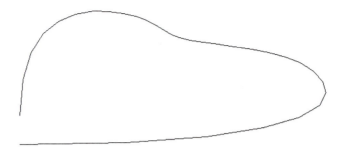

These unique lines have many uses in the various fields that use AutoCAD. For example, you can them for borders and title blocks, property lines, section cut lines, wall fill, and weighted lines.

See Also   For detailed instructions on the construction of polylines, and for examples of how they can be used in a drawing, see Sybex's beginner's book on AutoCAD, *AutoCAD 2000, No Experience Required*, by David Frey (this author!) or their comprehensive tome, *Mastering AutoCAD 2000*, by George Omura.

Splines—a Glimpse

Spline

Any curve that is defined by a set of control points, the placement of which will allow you to manipulate the shape of the curve.

AutoCAD offers the Spline command for drawing **spline** curves. Splines are irregular curves that are not based on arcs but on a series of control points that can be moved to control the shape of the curves. These curves are often used in laying out roads, paths, or other smooth shapes.

1. Start the Spline command by clicking the Spline icon on the Draw toolbar.

The drafter usually lays out a series of points and then passes the spline curve through those points to create a curve.

2. Click to choose the first point on the screen, and then move the crosshair away toward the next point.

At the beginning, the Spline commands looks like the Line command, or any other command that has rubber banding.

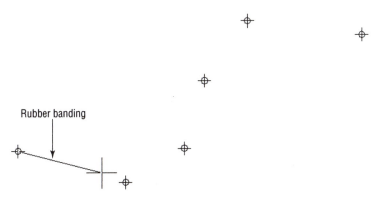

Rubber banding

3. When you pick the second point and move the line away from that point, the spline begins, and there is a new rubber-banding line.

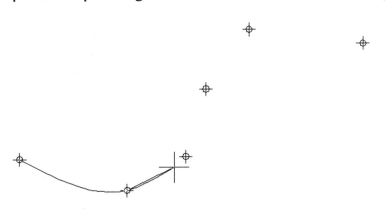

4. As you pick more points, the curve continues to change.

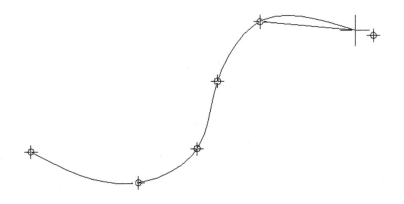

59

Tangent

To be in line with. Here, a rubber-banding line becomes tangent to the last or first part of a spline curve.

5. When you pick the last point, press ↵. A rubber-banding line appears that is **tangent** to the first part of the curve, and changes the beginning of the curve as you move the cursor.

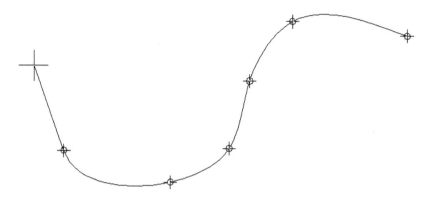

6. After you pick a point to establish the first tangent direction, another rubber-banding line appears, this time tangent to the end of the curve.

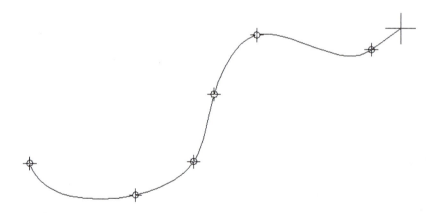

Grips

Small squares that appear on strategic points of lines and other items. They are used to quickly modify lines in a set number of ways.

7. When you pick the next point, the tangent direction for the end of the curve is established, the spline is complete, and the Spline command ends.

See Also   The shape of a spline curve can be modified by moving the control points, or **grips**, that it has passed through. For more on grips, see Chapter 8: "Selecting Items in Your Drawing."

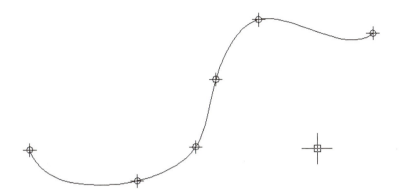

8. Using the Offset command, the new curve can be offset on either side to make a roadway.

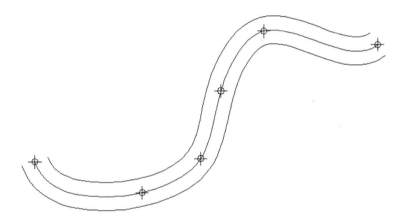

See Also The Offset command is discussed in Chapter 4.

Summary

In this chapter, you have looked at 11 of the commands that are used to draw new lines and shapes. There are 16 commands on the Draw toolbar and 21 on the Draw pull-down menu, and I encourage you to experiment with some of the ones not covered here. You will look at one other Draw command—Text—in Chapter 12: "Putting Text into a Drawing." Chapter 4 looks at some basic commands for modifying lines and other items already in a drawing.

Chapter 4

Making Changes

Many of the most-used commands in AutoCAD are those that change existing objects. About ten of these are basic commands that you will be learning in this chapter. All of them are on the Modify toolbar. They can be divided into two groups:

- ◆ Commands for modifying your drawing

- ◆ Commands for creating new lines from existing lines

Because the commands covered in this chapter all involve working with objects that already exist in the drawing, the examples start with drawings that contain a few simple objects. Feel free to re-create these drawings, or use any similar drawings you may have available, if you want to try out the exercises.

Objects

The lines, arcs, circles, text, and all other visible items in an AutoCAD drawing. Each type of object has unique properties as well as those in common with all objects, and is created by an individual command, such as the Line command for lines, and the Circle command for circles.

Modifying Your Drawing

The commands for modifying lines operate in similar ways: they all require you to select **objects** to be modified—though at different times—and they all require some other action to complete the command. The commands in this category are

- Erase
- Move
- Rotate
- Scale
- Trim
- Extend
- Fillet

You'll find these and the other commands covered in this chapter on the Modify toolbar:

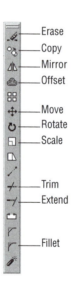

Erasing Lines

Erasing in AutoCAD is a three-step process: you start the Erase command, select the lines or other objects you want to erase, and then give the OK to erase them.

See Also   Chapter 8 is a complete guide to AutoCAD's tools and methods for selecting lines and other objects. To try out the techniques in this chapter, you can use the simplest selection method, left-clicking an object when the cursor appears as a pickbox.

1. Click the Erase button on the Modify toolbar to start the Erase command.

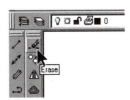

2. The crosshair changes to a pickbox. Move the pickbox to a line you want to erase, and then click once. The line will **ghost** to let you know it's been selected. Keep doing this to select more lines.

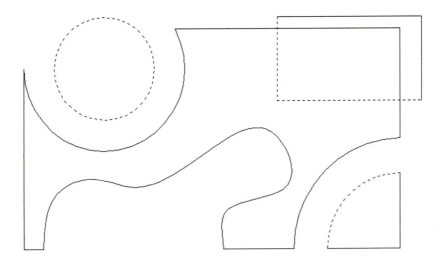

3. Press the Enter (⏎) key. The selected items disappear, and the Erase command ends.

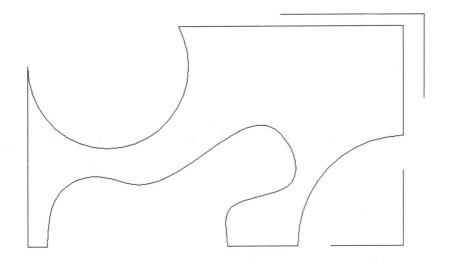

Moving Lines

In AutoCAD, you move items by specifying two reference points: the starting and ending points of the move. You can move a single item or several together. The items you select will move as you move the crosshairs across the screen.

1. Click the Move button on the Modify toolbar to start the Move command.

Pick

To place the pickbox on a line or other object and left-click to select it.

2. **Pick** the item or items to be moved. They ghost when selected.

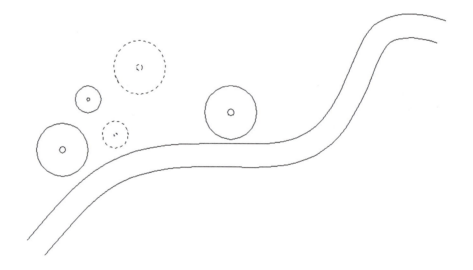

3. Press ↵ to finish selecting, and then pick a point somewhere in the middle of the selected item or items. Move the cursor away from the point you just picked. The selected items move with the cursor.

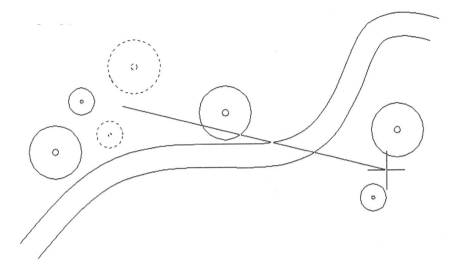

4. When the selected items are positioned where you want them to be, click. The move is complete and the Move command ends.

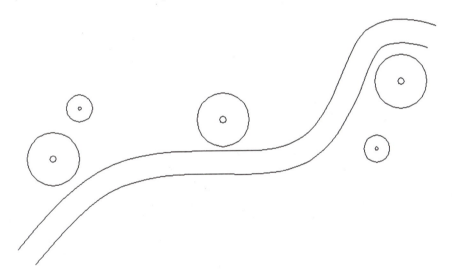

See Also To learn how to draw lines a specific distance and direction, see Chapter 6: "Working with Distances and Directions."

Rotating Lines

You can use the Rotate command to rotate a line or group of lines around a point that you choose.

1. Pick the Rotate button on the Modify toolbar to start the Rotate command.

2. Select the items in your drawing that you wish to rotate, and press ↵.

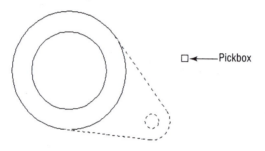

Pickbox

3. Pick a point about which you want the selected items to rotate.

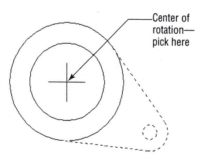

Center of rotation— pick here

Center of rotation

The point that selected lines rotate around. The center of rotation can be on one of the selected items but does not have to be.

4. Move the crosshair away from the point you just picked and then move it around that point. The selected objects rotate as the crosshair moves around the **center of rotation**.

5. Type in an **angle of rotation** in degrees, and press ↵.

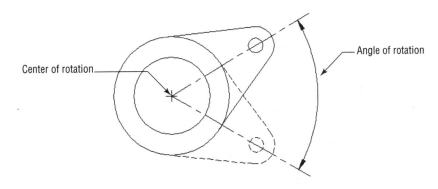

Center of rotation

Angle of rotation

Angle of rotation
The extent that objects rotate around the center of rotation, in degrees.

The counterclockwise direction of rotation is positive. Clockwise is negative.

6. The rotation is completed and the Rotate command ends.

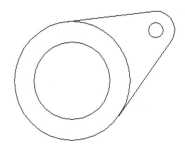

Scaling

The Scale command allows you to enlarge or shrink selected items. You control the magnitude of scaling by entering a **scale factor**.

Scale factor
A number that controls how much an object grows or shrinks with the Scale command.

1. Pick the Scale button on the Modify toolbar to start the Scale command.

The ruler has been placed in the picture to show how the scale command works. Normally, it won't be part of your drawing.

2. Select the items in your drawing that you wish to scale up or down, then press ↵.

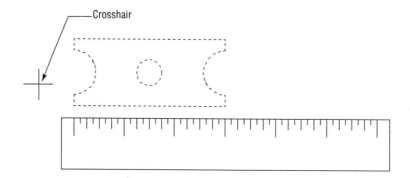

Base point

The point that items will move toward or away from when being scaled. Its location remains fixed.

3. Pick a point that will serve as the **base point**.

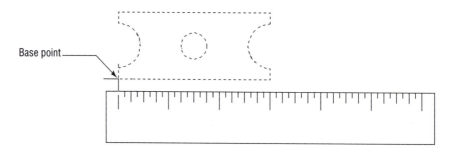

4. Move the crosshair away from the point you've just picked. The scaling changes with the movement of the crosshair.

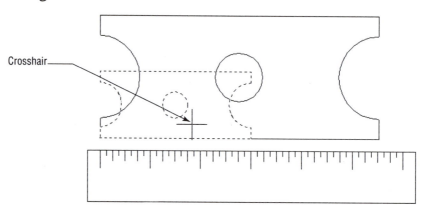

5. Type in the scale factor (in the example, the scale factor is 2 to make the object twice as big), or pick a point to set the scale. The selected lines will be scaled, and the Scale command ends.

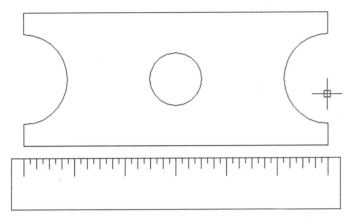

A scale factor must be a positive number, but it can be a decimal or fraction. Scale factors between 0 and 1 will scale down (or make smaller), and scale factors greater than 1 will scale up (or make larger).

Trimming

You can shorten lines to a reference line with the Trim command. AutoCAD calls the reference line a **cutting edge** when you are trimming, because it acts like a knife to cut lines.

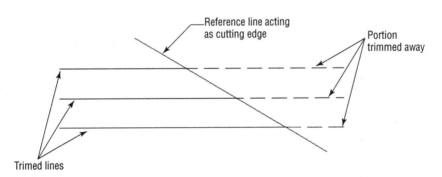

Cutting edge
A line that defines where selected lines will be cut.

1. Pick the Trim button on the Modify toolbar to start the Trim command.

You must press ↵ after you've picked the cutting edge, before you start trimming lines.

2. Select the line that will serve as a cutting edge. It will ghost. Then press ↵. The crosshair cursor changes to a pickbox, allowing you to select objects.

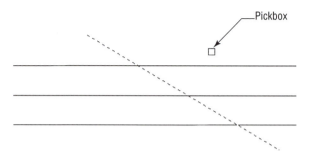

3. Pick the part of each line that is to be trimmed back to the cutting edge.

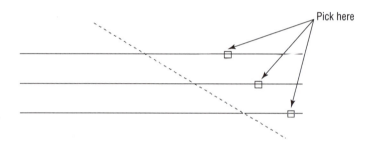

4. Press ↵ to complete the Trim command.

The Trim command will keep prompting you to pick lines to trim, until you press ↵ to end the command.

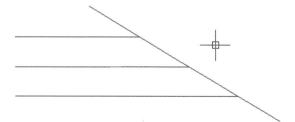

Note

You can select several lines as cutting edges, and lines that are to be trimmed can also serve as cutting edges.

Extending

Boundary edge
With the Extend command, a
line that selected lines extend to.

You can extend lines to a reference line with the Extend command. AutoCAD
calls the reference line for extending a **boundary edge** because it stops or limits
the extension.

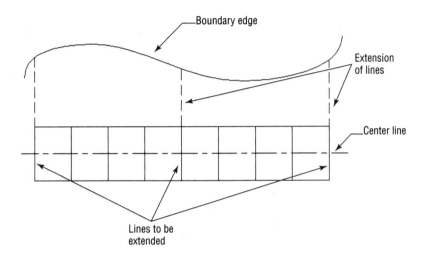

1. Pick the Extend button on the Modify toolbar to start the Extend command.

2. Select the boundary edge. It will ghost. Then press ↵.

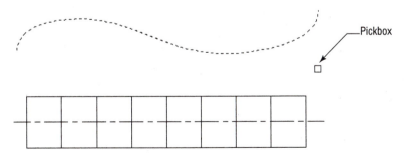

You must press ↵ after picking the boundary edge,
before you start picking lines
to extend.

3. Pick each line that you want to extend. Be sure to pick the half of the line that is nearest to the reference line.

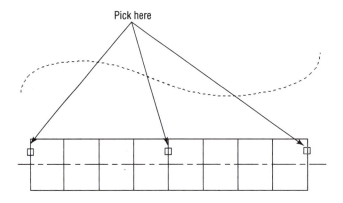

Pick here

The Extend command will keep prompting you to pick lines to extend until you press ↵ to end the command.

4. Press ↵ to complete the Extend command and turn it off.

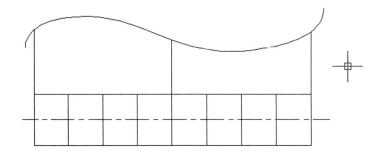

The Fillet command creates rounded corners, but if you set the corner radius to 0, it makes straight-edged corners. Fillet is used often with both 0 and non-0 radii.

Filleting to Clean Up Corners

Two lines that cross each other form a corner that may need to be cleaned up. You can do this cleanup with the Fillet command.

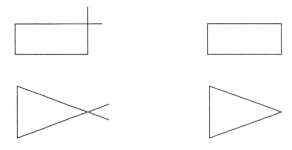

1. Pick the Fillet button on the Modify toolbar to start the Fillet command.

2. Check the Command window to see if the Radius is already set to 0. If it is, skip to Step 3. Otherwise, type **r** ↵, then type **0** ↵, and then press ↵ again to restart Fillet.

3. For each line, click once on the part that you want to keep.

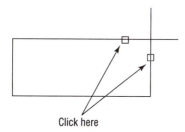

Click here

4. The cleanup is completed and the Fillet command ends.

 Tip

A corner can also be created by the Fillet command from any two lines that are not parallel, even if they don't intersect.

Pressing the Enter key at the Command prompt restarts the last command used.

Creating New Lines from Existing Lines

Several of the Modify commands create new objects from existing objects by various methods of copying. We will look at three of them: Copy, Mirror, and Offset.

Copying

The Copy command works just like the Move command, except that a copy of the original line or set of lines is moved to a new location in the drawing, and the original items stay put.

> AutoCAD also has the Windows Cut, Copy, and Paste tools on the Edit pull-down menu. These functions use the Windows Clipboard. By contrast, the Modify toolbar commands covered here do *not* use the Windows Clipboard. The Copy command on the Modify toolbar does *not* allow you to paste the lines being copied into another file.

1. Click the Copy button on the Modify toolbar.

2. Select the item or items to be copied. They ghost when selected.

See Also See Chapter 8: "Selecting Items in your Drawing" to learn more about the selection process in AutoCAD.

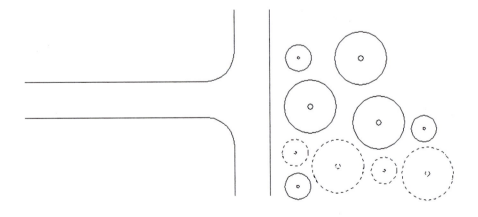

3. Press ↵, and then pick a point somewhere in the middle of the selected item or items. Then move the crosshair away from the point you just picked. A copy of the selected items moves with the cursor.

4. When the selected items are positioned where you want them to be, click. The copy of the selected items is placed and the Copy command ends.

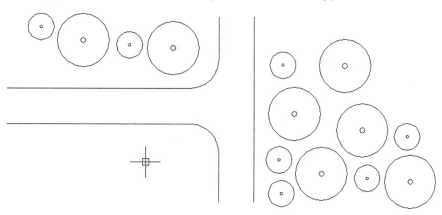

Tip

To make multiple copies of the selected items, type **m** ↵ after pressing ↵ in step 3 above. Then continue with step 4. When enough copies have been made, press ↵ again to end the Copy command.

See Also   To learn how to move items a specific distance and direction, see Chapter 6: "Working with Distances and Directions."

Mirroring

The Mirror command flips a line or group of lines about an axis. You then tell AutoCAD whether to keep the original line or delete it. As an example, you'll flip a partial cross-sectional view of a machine part around a center line to complete the view.

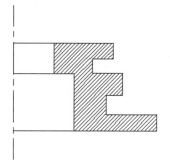

1. Pick the Mirror button on the Modify toolbar.

2. Select the items you wish to mirror, and then press ↵.

3. Pick a point in the drawing to start the **mirror line**. (In the example, I picked one end of the center line.) Then move the crosshair around. The flipped version of the selected lines moves as the movement of the crosshair changes the location of the mirror line.

Mirror line

The line that serves as an axis, around which selected lines are flipped to create a mirrored image.

By moving the crosshair around at this point, you can see where you want the mirror line to be positioned to get the results you want.

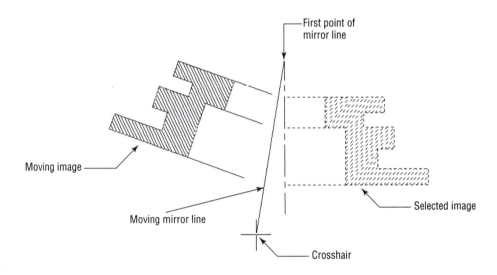

Moving image

First point of mirror line

Selected image

Moving mirror line

Crosshair

In some drawings, there may not be a convenient mirror line. You may have to construct a temporary line to serve as the mirror line.

4. Pick a second point to complete the mirror line in the drawing. (In the example, I picked the other end of the centerline.) The mirrored image disappears for a moment and the Command window displays a prompt that gives you the choice of whether to delete or keep the objects that were first selected.

```
Select objects:
Specify first point of mirror line: Specify second point of mirror line:
Delete source objects? [Yes/No] <N>:
```

5. Press ↵ to choose the **default** option of <N> (for No). The mirrored image is displayed along with the original and the Mirror command ends.

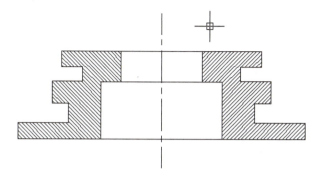

Offsetting Lines

The Offset command makes a specialized kind of copy of a selected line or shape. An **offset** line is a copy of a selected line that is placed a preset perpendicular distance away from the selected line. You can offset straight or curved lines, polylines, circles, and ellipses. For the example, you will offset a polyline.

See Also   See Chapter 3: "Drawing" to learn how to draw several kinds of lines.

1. Pick the Offset button on the Modify toolbar.

2. The Command window prompts you to enter a distance; enter an offset distance.

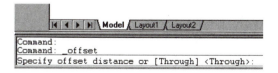

If you type **y** ↵ at the `Delete` prompt, AutoCAD keeps the mirrored copy and deletes the original lines that were selected. Use this option if you want to "flip" an object—make a mirror image of an existing item without keeping the original.

Offset
To create a copy of a selected item at a preset, perpendicular distance from the original.

The Offset command can also be started by typing **o** ↵, or by picking Modify ➤ Offset on the pull-down menus.

Enter **t** to select the `Through` option. This option asks you to first select the line to offset before you enter a distance. Then you are prompted to pick a point on the screen (the "Through point") to indicate the distance that the new line will be from the first line.

To offset a selected single line segment, you will pick to the right or left of it, or possibly above or below it.

3. Select the line (or lines) to be offset. They will ghost. Click on one side of the selected line or the other. This tells AutoCAD which direction you wish the offset to take. In the example, pick either inside the shape or outside it.

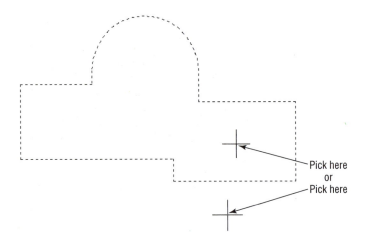

Pick here
or
Pick here

4. When you have picked a point, the offset occurs, and you are prompted to select another line to offset.

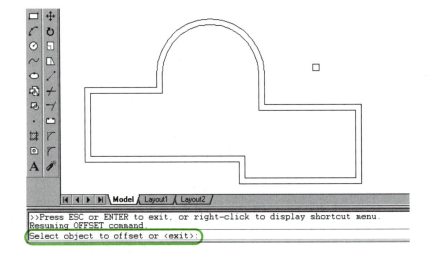

5. Repeat steps 3 and 4 until you are finished offsetting. Then press ↵ to end the Offset command.

Summary

This chapter has covered several of the basic commands used in AutoCAD to modify lines and other items in your drawing. As you gain confidence in using these commands, you will try some of those commands that weren't covered here and increase your proficiency in AutoCAD.

Part 2

Tools for Skilled Drawing

In addition to basic drawing and modification commands, AutoCAD has several features to help you draw specific layouts and geometrical patterns. Chapter 5 presents the minimal steps necessary to set up a new drawing. In Chapter 6, you will learn how to specify distances in a drawing. Chapter 7 presents the Object Snap Tools. These include a set of options for connecting lines to strategic points on other lines. Because so many of the modification commands require you to select lines to modify, it is useful to look at AutoCAD's features that aid you in the selection process, and we do this in Chapter 8. In Chapter 9 you will learn the basic methods for adjusting the view of your drawing on the screen. Finally, Chapter 10 discusses the essential tools for getting yourself out of trouble after a mistake has been made.

Tools for Skilled Drawing

Chapter 5

Setting Up a Drawing

When you start up a new drawing, there are a minimum number of settings that you will want to make sure are appropriate. This chapter shows how to set two of the most important:

- Drawing units
- Drawing size

Parameter

An independent variable in AutoCAD whose value usually has a default setting that can be changed by the user.

With AutoCAD already running, to start a new drawing, click File ➤ New. Then, in the Create New Drawing dialog box, click the Start From Scratch button and click OK. See Chapter 1 for more details.

Precision

The accuracy with which a number is displayed. In AutoCAD units, precision is set for the display of linear and angular measurement.

The Sample Output area at the bottom of the dialog box displays how the currently set linear and angular units, with the current precision settings, will appear.

Choosing the Drawing Units

The units that you choose for your drawing will determine the kind of distances and angles that will be entered to make lines a specific length. There are two types of units in AutoCAD: linear units for distances and angular units for rotational measure. Each type of unit has several options, but you will most likely use only one or two of these options for each type of unit.

Setting Linear Units

The setting for linear units is determined by the unit of measure that you are going to use for the distances in your drawing. We'll look at the choices as we set the linear units.

1. Start a new drawing by using the Start From Scratch option.

2. Pick Format ➤ Units to bring up the Drawing Units dialog box. Notice that the default setting for Length Type is Decimal and the **Precision** for Decimal is set to 0.0000.

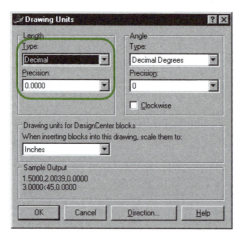

3. In the Length area, click the current Type (usually it is Decimal) to open the drop-down list that contains the choices for linear units.

4. In the list, click Architectural.

5. The drop-down list closes. Notice the precision setting for Architectural linear units. Click the Length Precision drop-down list to open it and see the choices for Architectural precision:

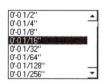

6. Click the 0'-0 $^1/_{16}$" precision choice to retain that setting and close the drop-down list. Leave the Drawing Units dialog box open if you want to set the Angular units. Otherwise click OK.

Note

The Precision setting for Units controls the accuracy with which a distance is displayed, but does not control the actual distance. For example, with a Precision setting of 0'-0 $^1/_4$", the length of a line that was precisely 1'-3 $^3/_{16}$" long would be displayed as 1'-3 $^1/_4$". This display is accurate to the nearest $^1/_4$".

This chart summarizes the five choices for linear units.

Linear Unit	Description	Example
Architectural	Uses feet, inches, and fractions	1'-6 $^1/_2$"
Decimal	Uses any decimal units	18.5 (inches) or 1.54 (feet) or 470 (mm)
Engineering	Uses feet, inches, and decimal inches	1'-6.5"
Fractional	Uses inches and fractions	18 $^1/_2$"
Scientific	Decimal with Exponential base	1.85E+01

Setting Angular Units

Angles or amount of rotation can be displayed in several ways in AutoCAD. If you still have the Drawing Units dialog box open from the previous exercise,

you can continue on with step 1 below. Otherwise, first open a new drawing and click Format ➢ Units before starting the following steps:

1. Take a look at the right side of the Drawing Units dialog box. The Angle Type is Decimal Degrees and the Precision is set to 0, or the nearest degree. Click on Decimal Degrees to open the Angle Type drop-down list and view the other options.

2. Click on Decimal Degrees to retain it or choose an alternative type; then click on the Angle Precision drop-down list to open it. Click on the desired precision.

3. Click OK to close the Drawing Units dialog box.

Specifying the Size of Your Drawing

When you start a new drawing, it is not necessary to set its size, because the electronic drawing on the computer has no size constraints. But since you will eventually print your drawing on a sheet of paper that *is* a specific size, you may find it useful to have a guide on the screen that helps you visualize your plan or layout on that sheet. Drawing limits and the grid will provide that guide. The next two sections examine both tools.

Setting the Drawing Limits

The Drawing Limits setting controls the width and length of the area in which you will be drawing. To define it, you specify two *x,y* **coordinates** that define the lower-left and upper-right corners of an imaginary rectangle on your screen.

The Precision settings control the display of a linear or angular measurement. See the note at the end of the preceding section.

By default, angles are measured positively in the counterclockwise direction and negatively in the clockwise direction.

Drawing unit settings are saved with each drawing, and can be changed at any time.

x,y **coordinate**
Two numbers, separated by a comma, that are the *x* and *y* values, respectively, for the location of a point on a grid that uses *x*- and *y*-axes. *X* represents the horizontal component and *y* the vertical.

See Also   Refer to Chapter 6: "Working with Distances and Directions" for more
about coordinate systems.

1. The AutoCAD drawing area has an invisible pair of *x* (horizontal) and *y* (vertical) **axes**. The position of every point on the screen is defined by an *x,y* coordinate.

Axes
The vertical and horizontal base lines for a x,y coordinate system.

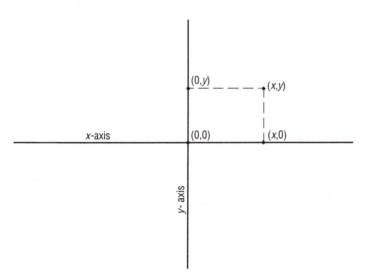

2. The drawing limits define the size of a rectangular area with two coordinates that serve as the lower-left and upper-right corners of the area. The lower-left coordinate is set to (0,0) by default. You will leave that as is, and set the coordinate for the upper-right corner to *x* and *y* values that describe an area large enough to encompass your drawing.

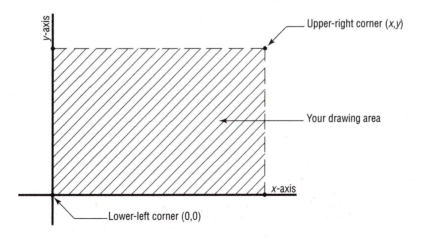

3. Say that you want to lay out a tennis court. It is 78 feet long and 36 feet wide. We will set the drawing limits to be a little larger than the tennis court dimensions to give ourselves a little extra room.

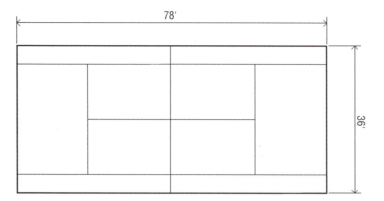

4. Click Format ➢ Drawing Limits and check the Command window. You are prompted to accept the default coordinate for the lower-left corner, or change it.

```
                   Model  Layout1  Layout2
Command: '_limits
Reset Model space limits:
Specify lower left corner or [ON/OFF] <0'-0",0'-0">:
```

5. Press ↵ to accept the default. The next prompt appears, this one for resetting the upper-right corner coordinate. The default is 12",9".

```
                   Model  Layout1  Layout2
Reset Model space limits:
Specify lower left corner or [ON/OFF] <0'-0",0'-0">:
Specify upper right corner <1'-0",0'-9">:
```

6. Type **100',50'**↵. The drawing limits have been set and the command ends.

To see the drawing limits, we need to display the AutoCAD grid. We'll do that in the next section.

The default drawing limits for a new drawing in Architectural units would define a drawing area that is 12 inches wide and 9 inches high.

When using Architectural units, you must type in the foot sign ('), but you don't have to type in the inch sign (").

Displaying AutoCAD's Grid

To see the limits that you set in the last section, you need to bring up the Auto-CAD grid. The grid is a rectangular **array** of dots with a set spacing, and it extends across the area defined by the drawing limits. (In the previous section, we set the drawing limits to 0,0 and 100',50'.)

1. Right-click on the Grid button on the Status bar.

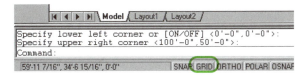

2. In the shortcut menu that appears, choose Settings. This brings up the Drafting Settings dialog box, with the Grid and Snap tab on top.

3. In the Snap Type & Style area, be sure Grid Snap and Rectangular Snap are selected.

4. The default Grid X & Y Spacing of ¹/₂" is obviously too small for a 100' × 50' drawing. Change those settings to 5'. Then place a check mark in the Grid On check box and click OK.

Array
An orderly pattern of objects. For the grid, the pattern is made up of rows and columns of dots.

The Grid and Snap settings are saved with your drawing.

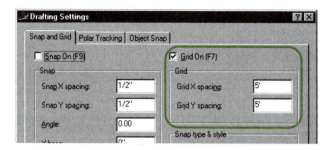

5. Type **z** ↵ **a** ↵. The grid appears on the drawing area.

The grid dots are a guide. They won't be printed with your drawing.

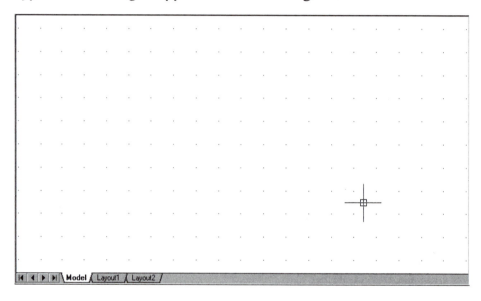

6. Click View ➢ Zoom ➢ Out. The grid gets smaller, and you can see its edges. These are the drawing limits you've defined.

You can display or hide the grid at any time by clicking the Grid button on the status bar.

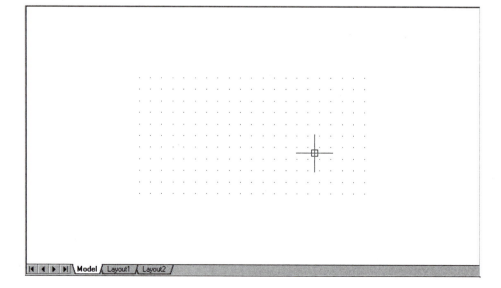

See Also   The zooming tools used in steps 5 and 6 are covered in detail in Chapter 9: "Controlling the View of Your Drawing."

Using the Snap with the Grid

You will sometimes have occasion to use the grid to help you draw. The cursor can be set to stop only at specific intervals of inches or feet, a feature called **snapping**. If you align this spacing with the grid spacing of its dots, you can draw by literally "connecting the dots."

1. For this exercise we'll use the setup from the previous two sections. Right-click the Snap button on the Status bar.

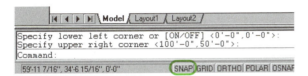

See Also   Snapping with the Snap tool is not the same as using Object Snaps. See Chapter 7.

2. In the Snap and Grid tab of the Drafting Settings dialog box, set the X and Y Snap Spacing to 5' (like the Grid spacing) and check the Snap On check box. Then click OK.

3. Move the crosshair cursor around on the grid and look at the Coordinate Readout window on the Status bar. The crosshair snaps from one grid point to another, and the coordinate readout shows that the coordinates are jumping at 5' intervals.

Snapping

A procedure for drawing with the Snap tool. Lines are all drawn to lengths that are multiples of the Snap spacing.

The snap and the grid can be set to different spacings. Sometimes the snap is set to a fraction of the grid. For example, you might use Snap: 1', Grid: 5'.

The snap and grid can be locked together. If the grid spacing is set to 0, then the snap spacing controls both the snap and grid spacing.

To lay out the tennis court that was shown in the previous section, you would start with a grid and snap spacing of 3' to lay out the 78' by 36' outside edge.

4. If you have an object to draw that has dimensions at 5' intervals, you can lay out the shape by using the Line command and snapping to the grid points.

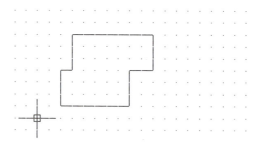

Note

Although the drawing limits, snap, and grid are helpful tools in setting up a drawing, they aren't essential. The only essential setup operation is to make sure the Units are set to the type you need.

Summary

With the setup variables covered in this chapter—units, drawing limits, snap, and grid—you now have the skills necessary to set up a new drawing to be of any size, and to see how that drawing will fit on your screen.

Chapter 6

Working with Distances and Directions

To do any kind of serious drawing in AutoCAD, you need to know how to tell the program what length a line should be, and in what direction it should be oriented. There are several tools in AutoCAD that help you specify lengths and angles, and we will examine them in this chapter:

- Direct distance entry
- The Ortho option
- Polar tracking
- The AutoCAD coordinate systems

Direct Distance Entry

Direct distance entry is a method of typing in distances for lines while at the same time using your cursor to control their direction. AutoCAD provides a couple of tools that allow you to control direction with your cursor.

Drawing Lines with Direct Distance Entry

See Also   See Chapter 5: "Setting Up a Drawing" for a discussion on units.

We will use a new drawing with decimal units for the illustrations.

1. Start the Line command and pick a point in your drawing.

2. Move the crosshair cursor away from the point picked, in the direction you want the line to be drawn.

3. Hold the crosshair still; then type in a distance and press ↵. (I used 4 for the direct distance entry.)

4. Repeat steps 2 and 3 a few more times. (I used 2.5, 4, and 2.5 for distances.)

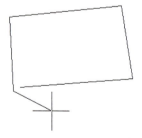

5. Press ↵ to end the Line command.

See Also   See Chapter 3 for help on the Line command and Chapter 4 for Erase.

Drawing Lines with Direct Distance Entry and Ortho

This time, we will use AutoCAD's Ortho option to force the lines you draw to be horizontal or vertical.

1. Click the Ortho button on the Status bar; then start the Line command and pick a point.

2. Move the crosshair cursor away from the point, to the right.

3. Type **4** ↵.

4. Hold the crosshair above the last endpoint.

5. Type **2.5** ↵. Hold the crosshair to the left of the last endpoint and type **4** ↵. Then type **c** ↵ to close the rectangle and end the Line command.

Drawing Lines with Direct Distance Entry and Polar Tracking

Polar Tracking gives you more flexibility than the Ortho option. While Ortho forces lines to be horizontal or vertical, with polar tracking, you can use a **tracking line** to help you draw lines at various preset angles.

1. On the Status bar, turn off Ortho and right-click the Polar button. Then click Settings on the shortcut menu.

Ortho is an On/Off toggle that you can also control with the F8 key.

When Ortho is on, the orientation—horizontal or vertical—of the next line segment is determined by the position of the crosshair cursor. When you move the crosshair around, you will see how the rubber-banding line jumps between horizontal and vertical.

Ortho can be turned on or off at any time, even in the middle of a command.

Tracking line
A temporary guideline that extends from a point and displays an option for the next line's direction. The crosshair with its rubber-banding line can be aligned with the tracking line.

2. In the Drafting Settings dialog box, make the following changes to the Polar Tracking tab, and then click OK:

   ◆ Put a check in the Polar Tracking On check box.

   ◆ In the Polar Angle Settings area, open the Increment angle check box and select 45.

   ◆ In the Polar Angle Measurement area, be sure Absolute is chosen.

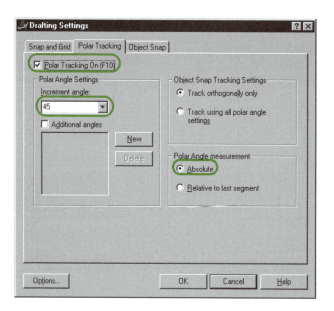

Note

You can also set your own custom angles for polar tracking. See Sybex's *Mastering AutoCAD 2000*, by George Omura.

Tracking ToolTip

The small text box that appears on the screen to help you identify the tracking line and its characteristics.

3. Start the Line command and pick a point to start a line. Move the cursor to a point directly to the right of the first point. Notice the tracking line that appears, with the **tracking tooltip** that sits next to the crosshairs.

4. When the tracking line is visible, type a distance in the Command window and press ↵. (I used 2 for a distance.)

5. Move the crosshair to a position about 45° above the horizontal, and to the right.

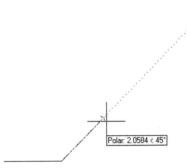

Polar tracking does not force the next line segment to a preset angle as Ortho does. It gives you the option to do so if the cursor is placed near enough to the preset angle.

6. When the tracking line and tooltip appear, the tooltip should read "< 45°". If it does, type in the next distance and press ⏎. (I used 2 again for the distance.)

7. Continue to repeat steps 5 and 6, each time using another tracking angle based on 45°, until you finish the shape. (For the example, I progressed in a counterclockwise direction at 45° increments, always using 2 as a distance.)

The '<' in the tracking ToolTip tells you that the number that follows is an angle. You'll learn more about this notation in "Using the Relative Polar Coordinate System," later in this chapter.

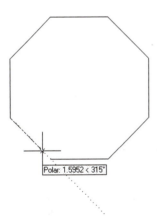

Note

This example uses the default orientation, in which a positive number represents counterclockwise rotation. A line pointing to the right has an angle of 0°; a vertical line is 90°, etc. See the later sections of this chapter for more on angle direction.

The AutoCAD Coordinate Systems

In AutoCAD you can use either the Cartesian or the Polar **coordinate system** for specifying distances and directions. Users generally prefer using one system or the other, but you need to know both. Each system is useful for certain situations, and sometimes the information you have at your disposal will dictate the choice of system. Both coordinate systems are illustrated in this section.

The Cartesian Coordinate System

The Cartesian system uses an ***x,y* coordinate** to designate how far horizontally and vertically the second point of a line is from the first point of that line. Directions up and to the right are positive, while down and to the left are negative.

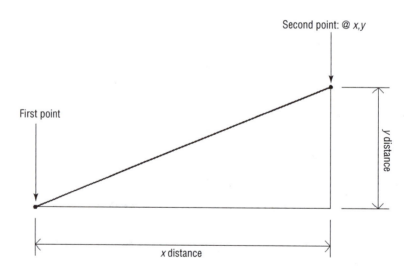

1. Start the Line command and pick a point on the screen.

2. Type in **@5,2** ↵. Note that 5 is the horizontal distance (*x*) between the first and second points, and 2 is the vertical distance (*y*) between those points.

The **@** symbol tells AutoCAD that the coordinate values following it represent distances from the last point specified. These are called *Relative Coordinates*.

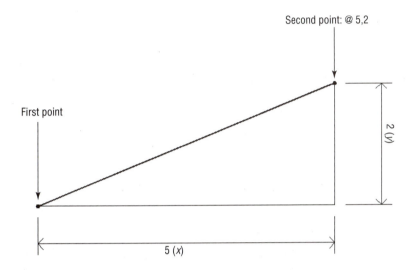

3. Press ↵ twice, once to end the Line command, and once to restart it and try another example. After picking the first point, type **@-5,2** ↵.

Negative *x* values designate distances to the left. Negative *y* values designate distances down.

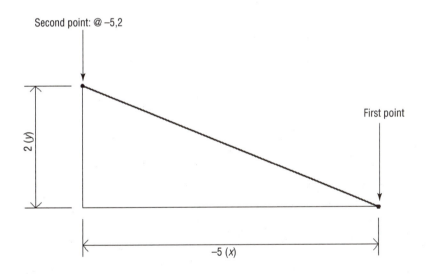

You can draw any shape this way if you know how far left or right, and up or down, the next point is from the last point.

4. The diagram shown below can be drawn using the Cartesian coordinate system. The coordinates that you would type in are shown.

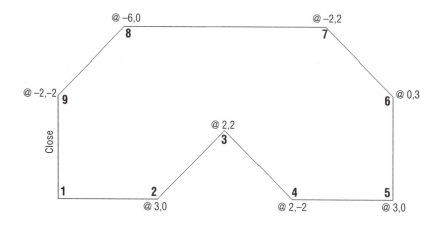

In AutoCAD, angles are measured positively in a counterclockwise rotation and negatively in a clockwise rotation.

The Polar Coordinate System

The polar coordinate system uses a distance and an angle to locate the next point of a line relative to the last point specified. Like the Cartesian system, the Polar system also uses the @ symbol, but it replaces the comma with the < symbol to designate that the number that follows is an angle and not the y coordinate. In the Polar system, distances are usually positive.

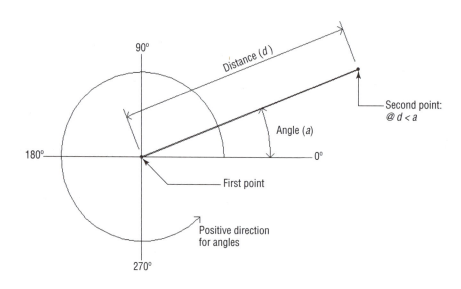

1. Start the Line command and pick a point.

2. Type **@5<22** ↵, where 5 is the distance from the first point to the second point, and 22 is the angle in degrees in a positive direction from the 0° direction, which is horizontal pointing to the right.

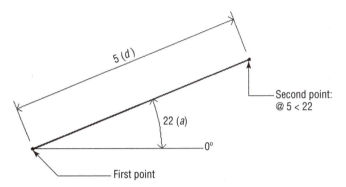

3. Press ↵ twice, once to end the Line command and once to restart it. Repeat steps 1 and 2, this time entering @5< 225.

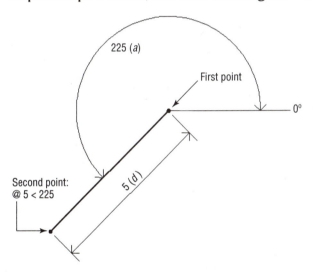

4. Try drawing the diagram shown below using the Polar coordinate system. The coordinates that you would type in are shown.

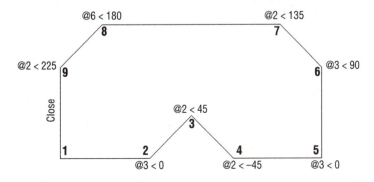

5. Many shapes require you to use a combination of polar and Cartesian coordinates. The choice of which you use depends on what information you have about the distances and directions between points.

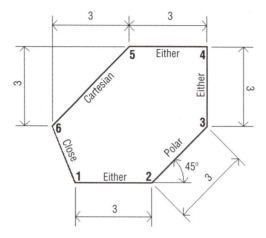

Summary

In this chapter, we have covered the five basic tools for specifying the length and direction of lines:

◇ Direct distance entry

◇ The Ortho option

◇ Polar Tracking

◇ The Cartesian coordinate system

◇ The Polar coordinate system

When you are comfortable using these drafting aids, you will be able to lay out shapes of any size.

Chapter 7

Achieving Precision with the Object Snap Tools

Lines, circles, and other items in AutoCAD drawings all have one or more strategic points that you can pick with the help of the Object Snap tools. In this chapter, you will learn about these tools and how you can use them to draw precisely and accurately. The Object Snap features covered in this chapter are:

◆ The most frequently used object snaps

◆ Selecting object snaps

◆ Turning on object snaps

◆ Temporarily disabling running object snaps

◆ Object snap and AutoSnap settings

◆ Object snap tracking features

Using Object Snaps

In Chapter 5, you learned about the Snap tool that works with the AutoCAD grid. Object snaps are individual tools that perform a similar function. But instead of snapping the lines you draw to points on the grid, they locate specific points in your drawing, such as the endpoint of a line or the center of a circle. Then you click the mouse to attach a line to that point. This is called "snapping" to a point.

Introducing the Basic Object Snap Tools

We can try out seven of the most frequently used object snap tools by drawing a series of line segments between various shapes in a diagram using these object snaps. To bring up the Object Snap toolbar and dock it above the drawing area, follow steps 1 and 2.

1. Bring up the list of available toolbars by right-clicking any toolbar button on the screen. Then select Object Snap from the list.

2. Move the Object Snap toolbar to the top of the drawing area and dock it under the Object Properties toolbar.

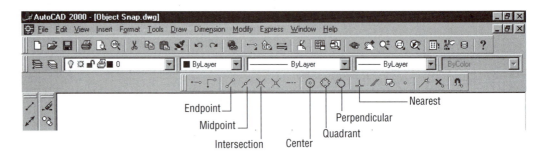

When an Object Snap tool has been picked, a symbol unique to that snap appears when you move the crosshair near a point it can snap to. For example, if Endpoint is selected and you move the crosshair to a line, a square appears at one or the other of the endpoints of the line.

See Also   See Chapter 1: "Starting Up AutoCAD 2000" for instructions on moving and docking toolbars.

To follow the remaining steps, you first need to draw the 8 lines, X, and circles that make up our diagram, as shown below. Then continue with step 3.

3. We'll start at the left and work to the right. Once you have the Line command running, click the Endpoint button on the Object Snap

toolbar. Then hold the crosshair near the right endpoint of the horizontal line at the left side of the diagram. When a small square appears at the endpoint, click. Your line will begin exactly at the endpoint.

4. Pick the Midpoint button from the Object Snap toolbar, then hold the crosshair near the middle of the short vertical line. When a small triangle appears at the midpoint of the line, click. The first segment of the line will end at the midpoint of the short vertical line.

5. Pick the Intersection button from the Object Snap toolbar and hold the crosshair near the intersection of the two sloping lines. When a small × icon appears at the intersection of the lines, click. The next segment of the line will end at the intersection that you just picked.

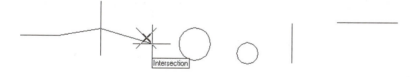

6. Pick the Center button from the Object Snap toolbar, and then hold the crosshair on the circle. When a small circle appears at the center of the circle, click. The next segment of the line will end at the center of the circle.

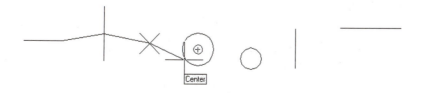

A command must be already started before you can select an object snap. They are not independent commands; instead, they work *with* commands.

The Intersection object snap will snap to where two lines cross, to where a line ends on a second line, or to where two lines end at the same point. There are several conditions in which you can use either Endpoint or Intersection object snaps, and some in which only one of them will work.

With the Center object snap, the small circle will appear at the center of the circle when you place the crosshairs near the circle or near its center. Also, when the small circle appears, a small + icon appears to identify the circle's center and will stay there until you left-click.

Quadrant point

Any of four points at the top, bottom, left, and right extremities of a circle or arc.

7. Pick the Snap to Quadrant button from the Object Snap toolbar, and then hold the crosshair near the top of circle. When a small diamond appears at the **quadrant point** at the top of the circle, click. The next segment of the line will end at the top of the circle.

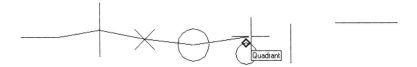

Osnap is short for Object Snap. You can see that Osnap is a toggle button on the status bar.

8. Pick the Perpendicular button from the Object Snap toolbar, and then hold the crosshair on the vertical line. When the Perpendicular symbol appears on the line, click. The next segment of the line will end at the line and be perpendicular to it.

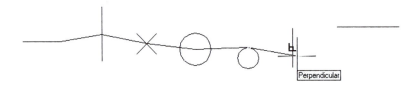

The Nearest object snap will snap to the point on a line that the crosshairs are nearest to at the time that you click.

9. Pick the Nearest button from the Object Snap toolbar, and then hold the crosshair on the arc. A small hourglass will appear on the line and move along the arc as you move the crosshair. When the hourglass is positioned about where you would like to end the line, click. The last segment of the line will end at the arc.

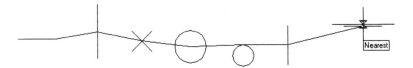

10. Press ↵ to end the Line command. The exercise is complete.

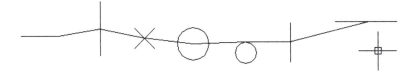

Setting Object Snaps to Be Running

You can set several of the object snaps that you use frequently to be **running**; that is, constantly selected. Once they are running, you will not have to select them each time you need to use them. If you choose to have snaps running, however, there are times when they can interfere with your work. We will learn how to temporarily disable running snaps later in the chapter.

1. Click the Object Snap Settings button on the Object Snap toolbar. The Drafting Settings dialog box appears, with the Object Snap tab active.

2. Put checkmarks in the check boxes next to the Object Snap modes that you wish to have running.

3. Put a check in the Object Snap On check box and click OK.

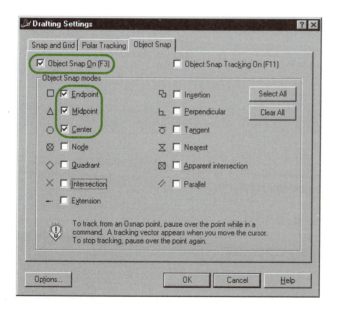

Now when you draw and need to use the object snaps that are running, you don't need to pick them. The symbols for the running object snaps automatically appear when the crosshair is placed near a line or circle.

Running
Active and ready to be used without being selected.

You can also bring up the Object Snap tab of the Drafting Settings dialog box by right-clicking on the Osnap button on the Status bar and then choosing Settings in the menu that appears.

Notice that the symbol assigned to each object snap is displayed to the left of its check box.

Running Object Snap settings are saved with the AutoCAD program and not with the currently active drawing.

When you have running object snaps, you can still pick a single object snap from the Object Snap toolbar. Once you pick one, the running object snaps are overridden for the next pick. Then they are restored after the pick.

Temporarily Disabling Running Object Snaps

You will occasionally find that you need to deactivate your running object snaps temporarily because they are interfering with what you are doing at the moment.

1. Left click on the Osnap button on the status bar to deactivate all running object snaps.

2. Left-click again on the Osnap button to reactivate the same running snaps you had previously set.

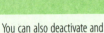

You can also deactivate and reactivate running object snaps by pressing the F3 key.

Deactivating All Object Snaps for One Pick

Once in a while you will want to pick a point in your drawing with no object snaps, but the running object snaps keep appearing and getting in your way. You can cancel all object snaps for one pick.

1. Start your drawing or modifying command and progress to the point where you need to turn off all object snaps for one pick.

2. Click the None icon on the Object Snap toolbar.

3. Pick the point on the screen, using no object snaps.

After one pick, the running object snaps are reactivated and will be available for the next pick.

The Object Snap Settings

You can control how object snaps behave and what is displayed on the screen when you use them.

1. Click the Object Snap Settings button on the Object Snap toolbar. The Drafting Settings dialog box appears.

2. Click the Options button. The Options dialog box appears with the Drafting tab displayed. There are seven settings that affect the appearance and behavior of the Object Snap tools.

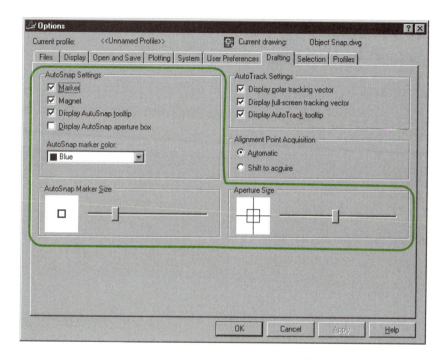

3. Among other things, you can control the visibility, size, and color of the Object Snap symbol (called an *AutoSnap Marker*) that appears near the crosshair cursor. Make necessary changes and click OK.

4. Back in the Drafting Settings dialog box, click OK.

A Tour of the Object Snap Tracking Features

Object snap **tracking** is similar to polar tracking—discussed in Chapter 6: "Working with Distances and Directions"—in that both display guidelines on the screen to which you can attach the crosshair as a guide to pick the next point. While polar tracking shows guidelines—called **tracking lines**—at preset angles from the last point picked, object snap tracking shows tracking lines extending horizontally

Changes you make to Object Snap settings are saved with the AutoCAD program, and not with the drawing.

Tracking

A process of specifying the location of points relative to the location of other points in the drawing.

Tracking line

A temporary guideline that extends from a point and displays an option for the next line's direction. The crosshairs with their rubber-banding line can be aligned with the tracking line.

and vertically from object snap tracking points on lines and other geometric figures. In general the Tracking feature minimizes the need to enter data on the keyboard by providing preset guidelines instead.

Using Object Snap Tracking Points

When you have set object snaps to be running, you can use the running snap points on lines as temporary **tracking points.** These points are then used to set up tracking lines as an aid to locating new points in the drawing. It sounds complicated, but it isn't. The example will illustrate.

Tracking points

Locations in your drawing that are temporarily used as the base of a guideline (tracking line). They are indicated by a small cross icon, which appears when the crosshairs are momentarily rested at the location.

1. On the Status bar, right-click on Otrack and choose Settings from the shortcut menu.

2. In the Object Snap tab of the Drawing Settings dialog box, place check-marks in the following check boxes:

   ◇ Object Snap On

   ◇ Object Snap Tracking On

   ◇ Endpoint

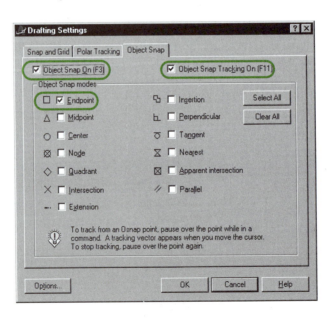

3. On the Status bar, the Osnap, Otrack, and Model buttons will be the only buttons that are depressed.

4. In the drawing, with the Rectangle command started, place the cursor on the upper-right corner of the lower rectangle and hold it there for a moment until a small + icon appears at the corner. Don't click the mouse yet. As the crosshair is moved to the right, a horizontal tracking line appears.

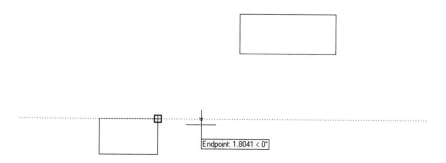

5. Move the crosshair cursor to the lower-left corner of the upper rectangle and hold it there until a + icon appears at the corner. Don't click a mouse button yet.

6. Move the crosshair down from the corner and note the vertical tracking line that appears.

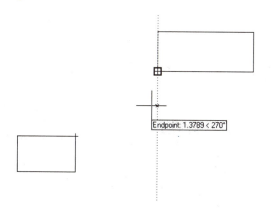

Once a tracking point cross appears, you can make it disappear by holding the crosshair briefly on it a second time.

7. Keep moving the crosshair down until it lines up horizontally with the tracking point from the lower rectangle. Its tracking line appears, and the two tracking lines now intersect at the point where you want to start a new rectangle.

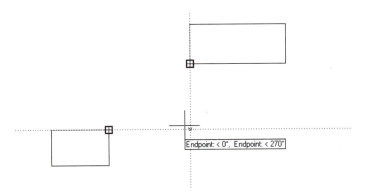

8. Click to start the first corner of the new rectangle.

9. Repeat steps 4 through 7 to use object snap tracking to establish the second corner of the new rectangle.

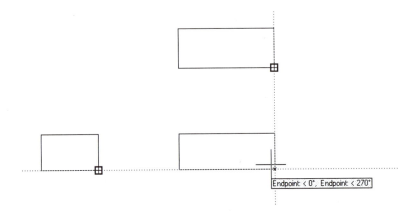

10. Click to complete the rectangle and end the Rectangle command.

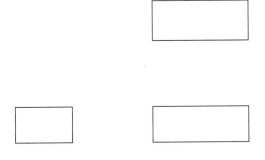

Summary

This chapter has introduced seven of the most frequently used object snaps and showed how adjusting their settings can control their behavior. Then you saw how the object snaps can be used in various tracking modes. You'll learn more about object snaps as you begin exploring AutoCAD on your own. For more comprehensive discussions on object snaps and object snap tracking, I refer you to Sybex's *Mastering AutoCAD 2000*, by George Omura, or to *AutoCAD 2000: No Experience Required*, by this author, and also a Sybex book.

Chapter 8

Selecting Lines and Other Items in Your Drawing

Any time you are using a Modify command, you will need to select those lines or other objects in your drawing that you intend to modify; so it helps to have an idea of the basic selection tools and selection options that are at your disposal. This chapter looks at the selection process in two parts. The first part introduces the basic tools for selecting lines and other items in your drawings, and illustrates why these tools are important. The second part looks at the three different ways in which in which you can use the selection tools in AutoCAD.

- ◆ Selecting with windows

- ◆ Selecting with special lines

- ◆ Undoing selections

- ◆ Selecting everything in your drawing

- ◆ Selecting before choosing a modify command

- ◆ A quick look at grips

Selection Tools

Selection process

Any procedure that you may use for selecting a group of lines in a drawing so that they may be erased, moved, or otherwise modified.

Selection set

The group of one or more lines or other objects that have been selected through a selection process.

As you learn about the selection tools presented here, it will help your understanding if you think of the **selection process** as one of building up a **selection set**. Once the selection set is fixed, then you can perform the modification you intend on the selected items. In this section, I will illustrate the selection tools by modifying various parts of a partial floor plan. If you want to try these procedures on your own as exercises, you can use almost any simple drawing.

Picking Lines to Select Them

The easiest and quickest way to select one or two lines is to pick the lines.

1. Start the Modify command that you wish to use. You will see the `Select objects` prompt in the command window, and the crosshair cursor changes to a pickbox.

Anytime you see the pickbox in the drawing area, or the `Select objects` prompt on the bottom line of the command area, Auto-CAD is ready for you to select lines or other items in your drawing.

2. Move the pickbox onto a line you wish to modify, and then click. The line ghosts.

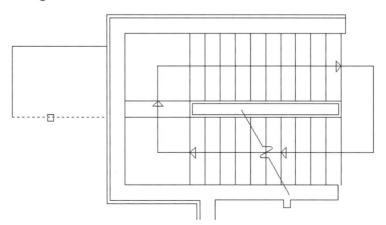

3. Continue this process to select other lines.

4. When you have selected all the lines you want to modify, press ↵. This will end the selection process and you will be prompted for the next step of the command.

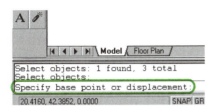

It is important to remember to press ↵ when you are finished selecting items to modify. If you don't, Auto-CAD expects you to select more items.

Making a Regular Selection Window

If you need to select more than two or three lines to modify, it may be convenient to use a window to select them. AutoCAD offers several types of selection windows. The **regular selection window** selects everything that's completely inside it.

Regular selection window
The selection tool that creates a window and selects everything inside it. On the prompt line that displays all the selection options, it's called simply "Window".

1. Once a Modify command has been started, and the pickbox is on the screen, pick a point in an open area of the screen below and to the left of the lines that you wish to select. Then move the cursor up and to the right to start defining the window.

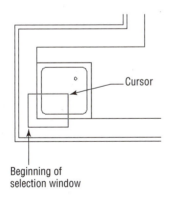

Cursor

Beginning of selection window

Tip

If the pickbox is too close to a line when you try to start a selection window, AutoCAD will select the line instead of starting the window. You might want to temporarily disable the object snaps, as discussed in the previous chapter, to minimize interference with the selection process.

2. Move the cursor up and to the right until all lines you wish to select are completely inside the window.

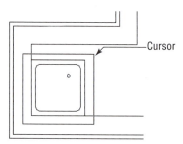

Cursor

3. Click to complete the selection window. Only the items that were entirely within the window have been selected.

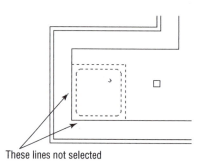

These lines not selected

4. Select other lines, or press ↵ to end the selection process, and continue on with the modify command that you have started.

Crossing selection window

The selection tool that creates a window and selects everything inside it and everything that crosses the four lines that make up the window's dashed boundary. On the prompt line that displays all the selection options, it's called "Crossing."

Tip

You can compel AutoCAD to create a regular selection window by typing **w** ↵ at the Select objects prompt. When this is done, you can form the window by moving the cursor in either direction—left or right. It may be convenient to create the window in this way if you find your drawing too cluttered at the spot where you would normally start the selection window. Again, temporarily disabling the object snaps may also simplify selection.

Making a Crossing Selection Window

Another kind of selection window is the **crossing selection window**; it will select everything inside the window and anything that crosses the window's bound-

ary line. You might use this tool when lines you want to select cross lines that you don't want to select.

1. Once a Modify command has been started, and the pickbox is on the screen, pick a point in an open area of the screen below and to the right of the lines that you wish to select. Then move the cursor up and to the left to start the window. Note that the lines of this window are dashed.

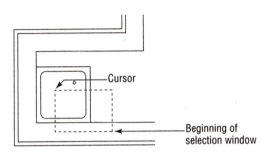

The crossing selection window is distinguished from the regular crossing window by its dashed boundary lines.

2. Move the cursor up or down and to the left until all lines you wish to select are completely inside the window or crossing one of the dashed border lines of the window.

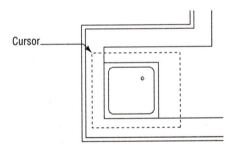

To make a crossing selection window, after the window is started, move the cursor to the left to form the window.

3. Click to complete the selection window. The items that were entirely within the window, plus the lines that cross the window's dashed boundary, have been selected.

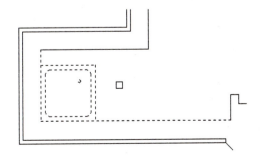

4. Select other lines or press ↵ to end the selection process, and continue on with the Modify command that you have started.

You can also create a crossing selection window by typing **c** ↵ and then moving the cursor right or left. Again, this technique may be useful if your drawing is cluttered.

Selecting Everything in the Drawing

When you need to select everything that is visible in your drawing for a modification, this is a simple operation.

1. Start the Modify command you intend to use on the entire drawing.

2. Type **all** ↵. All visible objects will be selected.

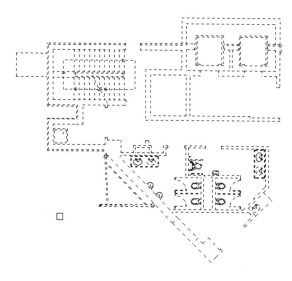

Using the All option is similar to making a selection window around your whole drawing.

3. If there are objects in your drawing you don't want to modify, deselect them now (as described later in this chapter). Otherwise, press ↵ to end the selection process and continue with the Modify command you have started.

Sometimes it's more efficient to select everything in your drawing and then deselect the specific items that don't need modifying.

See Also   Using the All option selects objects on any layers that have been turned off, as well as all visible objects. See Chapter 11: " Working with Layers and Properties," for more information about layers.

Using a Fence to Select Lines

The fence is a selection tool that behaves like the boundary of a crossing selection window. It is a line segment, or a series of continuous line segments, that selects everything it crosses.

1. Start the Modify command that you wish to use.

2. At the Select objects prompt, type **f** ↵.

3. Pick points to make one or more line segments that cross the lines you wish to select.

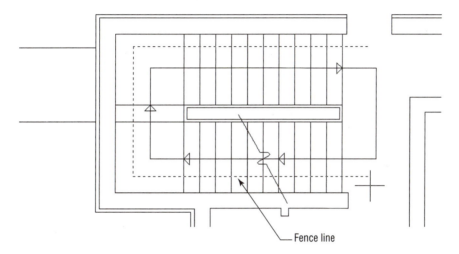

Fence line

Fence lines can be one segment or any number of connected segments.

4. When the fence crosses all lines you want, press ↵. The crossed lines are selected.

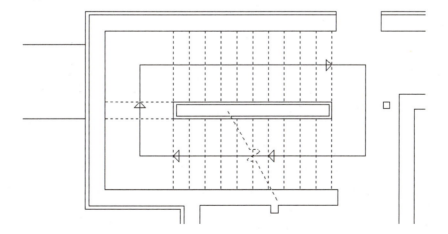

After using a fence line, you can then use other selection options.

5. Use other selection options if necessary.

6. Press ↵ to end the selection process and continue on with the Modify command that you have started.

123

See Also   Fence lines can also be used to remove lines from a selection set. See the next section.

Removing Items from the Selection Set

Often, the selection process will require more than one selection option. It may be most efficient to select more lines than you actually want to modify, and then remove the ones that you don't want from the selection set.

1. Start the Modify command that you want to use.

2. Start a regular selection window around an area that contains the lines you want to modify.

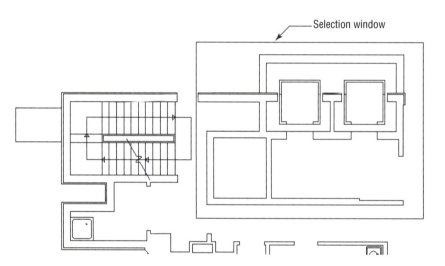

Selection window

3. Complete this window.

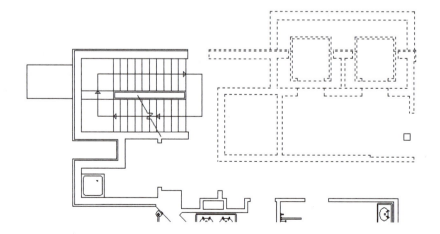

4. Type **r** ↵. This starts the **remove process**. Notice that you now have a `Remove objects` prompt.

5. Start a regular selection window around a group of lines you wish to remove from the selection set.

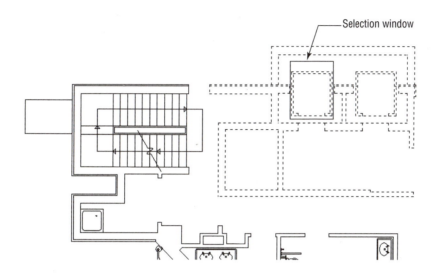

Selection window

6. Complete this window.

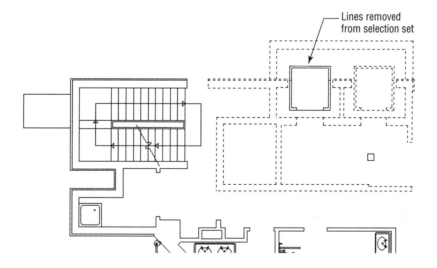

Lines removed from selection set

7. Make another window to remove more lines, if necessary.

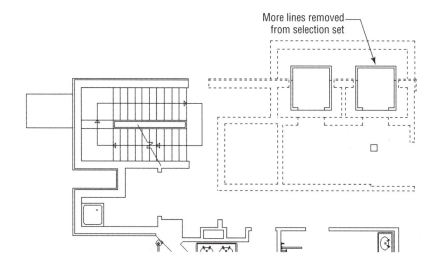

More lines removed from selection set

8. Press ↵ to end the selection and removal process, and to continue on with the Modify command that you have started.

You can also use any of the selection options—like a crossing window or picking—to remove lines from a selection set.

Reselecting the Previous Selection Set

If you have just selected lines and performed a Modify command on them, you can reselect the last selection set for use with another Modify command.

1. Start the next Modify command.

2. At the `Select objects` prompt, type **p** ↵. The previous group of selected items is reselected.

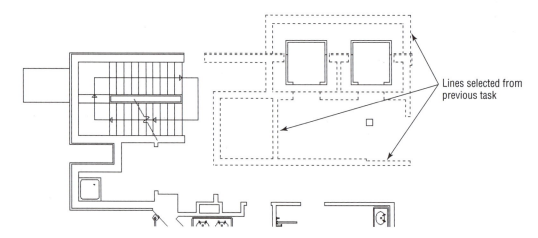

Lines selected from previous task

3. Continue the selection process, or press ↵ to end selection.

4. Complete the steps for the Modify command that you started in step 1.

126

How the Selection Process Works

The selection process works in two different ways. You can select lines or other objects after starting a command, as discussed in the previous sections; but you can also make your selections before starting a command.

The first three selection tools that were discussed in the previous section—picking, regular window, and crossing window—are available in both of the selection processes. The rest of the selection tools we've discussed can be used only when you are selecting lines after a command has been started. When you select objects first, however, you also have another tool: selection grips.

Selecting Lines After a Command Has Been Started

This method of selecting lines is the most basic, and was used to illustrate the selection tools in the previous section. All selection tools are available for this method.

1. First, a Modify command is started.

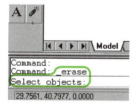

2. Then selection takes place.

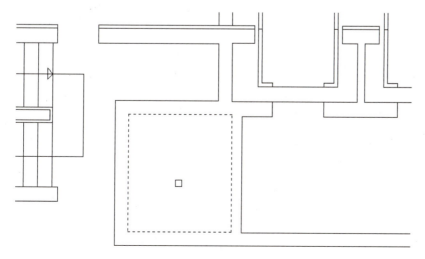

For any complicated selection process, this method of selection will be used because it allows the use of all selection tools. When you select objects first, many of the selection options aren't available.

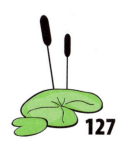

127

3. When the selection set is finalized, press ⏎ to end the selection process and continue on with the Modify operation you have started.

Selecting Lines Before a Command Has Been Started

You can also select lines or other objects before starting some of the Modify commands. Six of the Modify commands illustrated in Chapter 4 can be used by selecting lines first: Erase, Copy, Mirror, Move, Rotate, and Scale. When using this selection method, you can use picking, Regular selection windows, and Crossing selection windows.

Grips

Small squares that appear on strategic points of lines and other items. They are used to quickly modify lines in a set number of ways.

1. Use picking, a regular selection window, or a crossing selection window to select lines to be modified. Note that lines selected are ghosted and display small squares on them, called **grips**.

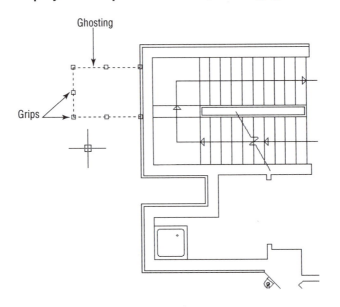

The option to select objects before starting a command can be disabled by clicking Tools ➤ Options ➤ Selection tab and then unchecking the Noun/Verb Selection check box in the Selection Modes area.

2. When finished selecting, start a Modify command.

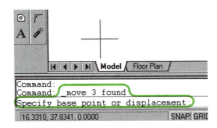

3. Continue the steps to complete the Modify command that you just started.

See Also Sometimes you will accidentally select lines when no command is running. If this happens, press the Esc key twice to remove the ghosting and the grips. See Chapter 10: *Correcting Errors*.

Using Grips with a Selection Set

When you select lines before starting a Modify command, small squares called grips appear on the lines. These grips allow you to use any of six modify commands without having to select them from the Modify toolbar: Stretch, Move, Copy, Rotate, Scale, and Mirror.

1. Use picking, a regular selection window, or a crossing selection window to select lines to be modified.

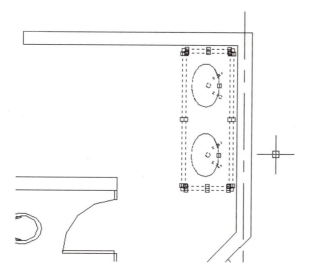

To control the color of inactive and active grips, click Tools ➤ Options ➤ Selection tab. For inactive grips, yellow is good for a black background, and blue is good for a white background. Red is usually a good color for the active grip.

2. Click on a grip to activate it. The grip will change to a solid color.

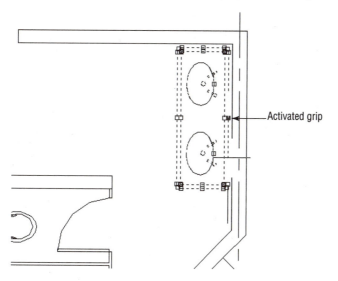

Activated grip

Once a grip has been activated, you can right-click to bring up a shortcut menu that has the grip options on it. This is an alternative to using the space bar to cycle through the grip options.

You can press the Esc key several times while using grips, to cancel what you are doing and remove the grips.

3. In the Command window, the Stretch command has already started. Press the space bar to cycle through the five Modify commands that work with grips, until you come to the one you want to use.

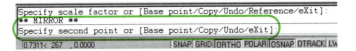

4. Type **c**↵ to start the Copy option.

5. Follow the prompts for the command to complete it.

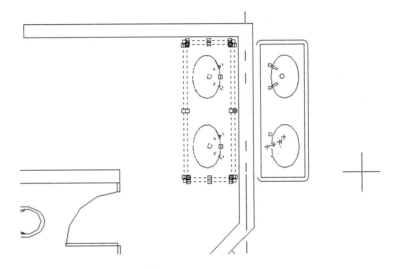

6. Press the Esc key twice to remove the grips.

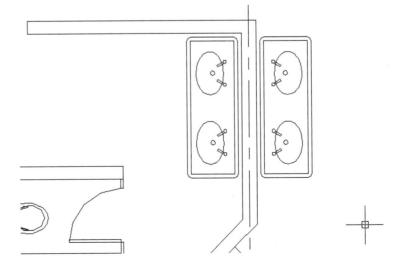

An AutoCAD Gallery

The following examples of AutoCAD drawings have been contributed by professionals who have been using AutoCAD anywhere from a year or two to many years. We've included a little information about each drawing's real-world purpose; but for the most part, these AutoCAD examples speak for themselves.

Jonathan Zimmerman, Architect

Jonathan Zimmerman, Architect, uses AutoCAD to design monolithic concrete domes that are used as residences and commercial facilities. He finds the geometrical precision of AutoCAD to be very helpful in calculating the complex curves that are generated by the shape of the concrete shell.

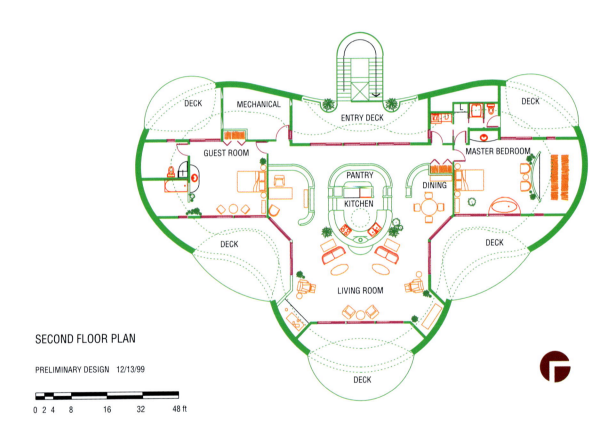

SECOND FLOOR PLAN

PRELIMINARY DESIGN   12/13/99

0 2 4   8   16   32   48 ft

The first example is the second-floor plan of a hurricane-resistant residence designed for a private island, with numerous decks to take advantage of dramatic views of the site.

Jonathan Zimmerman, Architect

This large, ellipse-shaped dome is used for recreation. It houses half a basketball court.

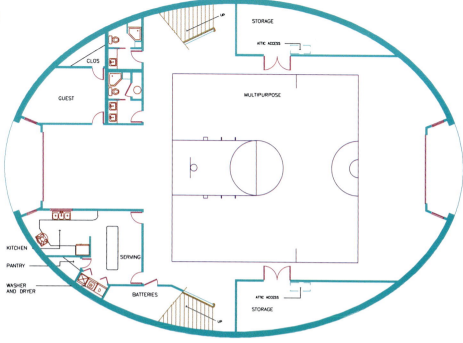

FIRST FLOOR PLAN

The last example of Jonathan's work with concrete domes is a guest house that sits among a large complex of dome structures.

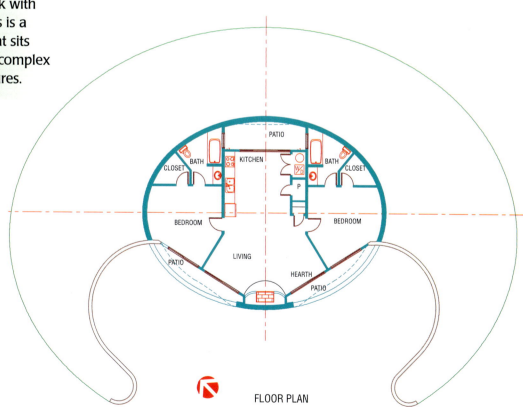

FLOOR PLAN

Jonathan Zimmerman, Architect

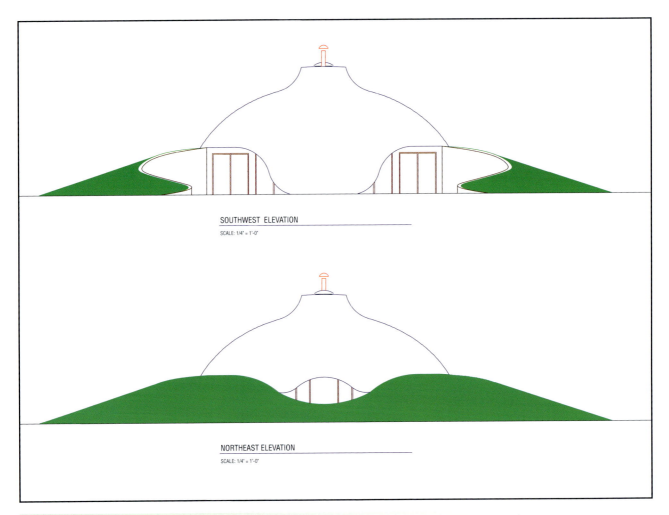

SOUTHWEST ELEVATION

SCALE: 1/4" = 1'-0"

NORTHEAST ELEVATION

SCALE: 1/4" = 1'-0"

These exterior elevations illustrate a new concrete dome shape for the guest house.

Jonathan Zimmerman, Architect

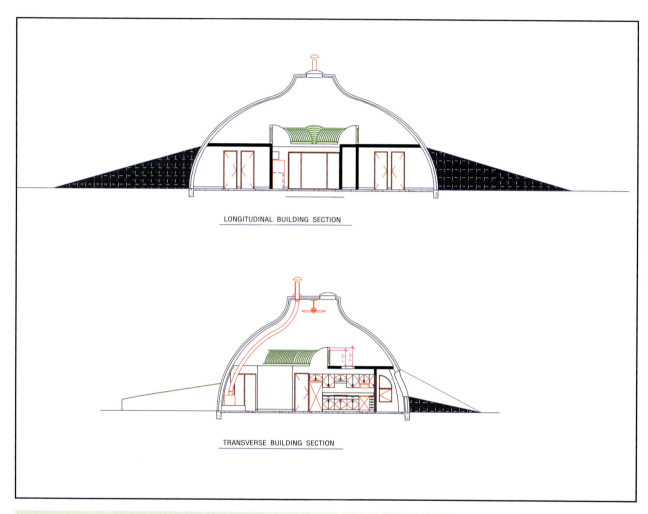

LONGITUDINAL BUILDING SECTION

TRANSVERSE BUILDING SECTION

Guest house building sections with interior elevations.

Jonathan Zimmerman, Architect

MetlSaw Systems, Inc.

Jim Schlacter at MetlSaw Systems, Inc. contributed the following set of mechanical drawings that delineate various parts that are assembled into the large, industrial metal-cutting saws that MetlSaw designs and makes. Many of the parts are standardized and then slightly altered for each custom-built machine. Jim finds AutoCAD to be a great tool for controlling the design of these parts.

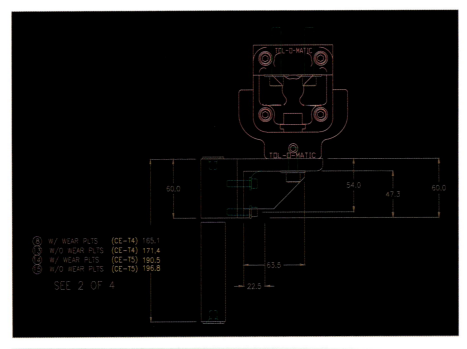

End view of side clamp assembly with mounting bracket

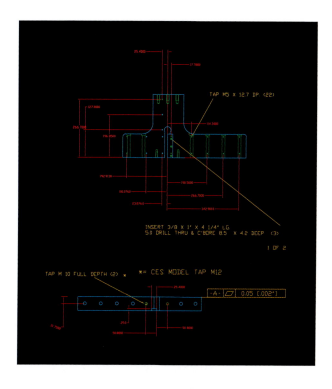

Squaring fence (right);
assembly diagram of
chain dampener (below)

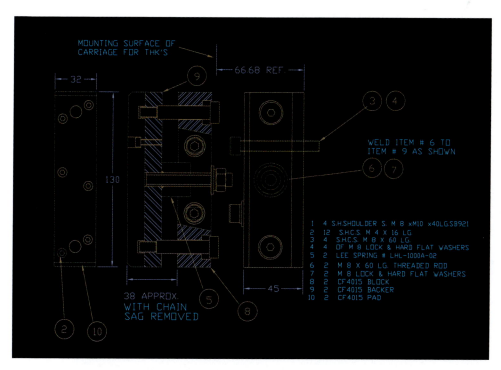

MetlSaw Systems, Inc.

Support frame profile (top); flame cut template (bottom)

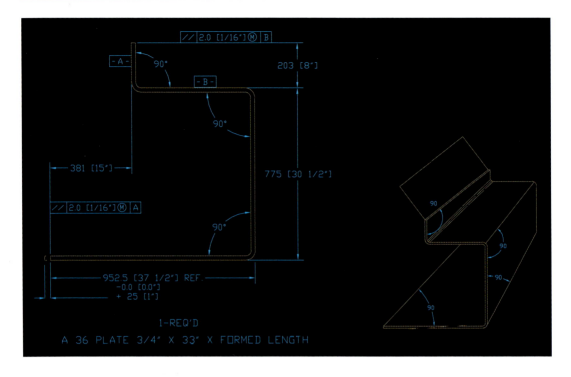

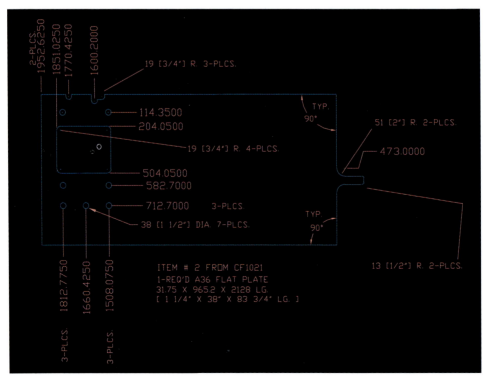

MetlSaw Systems, Inc.

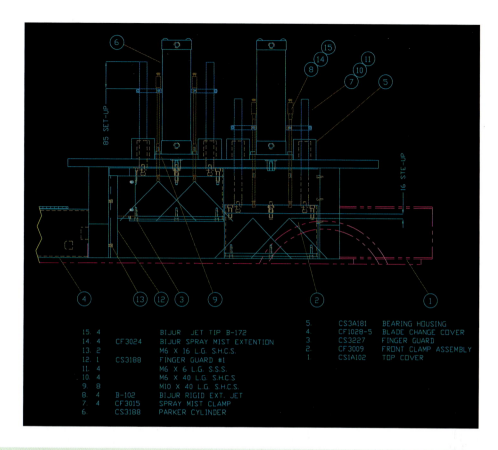

15. 4		BIJUR JET TIP B-172
14. 4	CF3024	BIJUR SPRAY MIST EXTENTION
13. 2		M6 X 16 L.G. S.H.C.S.
12. 1	CS3188	FINGER GUARD #1
11. 4		M6 X 6 L.G. S.S.S.
10. 4		M6 X 40 L.G. S.H.C.S.
9. 8		M10 X 40 L.G. S.H.C.S.
8. 4	B-102	BIJUR RIGID EXT. JET
7. 4	CF3015	SPRAY MIST CLAMP
6.	CS3188	PARKER CYLINDER

5.	CS3A181	BEARING HOUSING
4.	CF1028-5	BLADE CHANGE COVER
3.	CS3227	FINGER GUARD
2.	CF3009	FRONT CLAMP ASSEMBLY
1.	CS1A102	TOP COVER

Material clamp beam assembly with pneumatic clamps (top); top view of saw assembly (below)

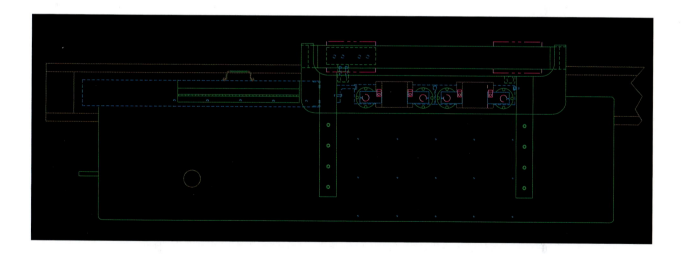

MetlSaw Systems, Inc.

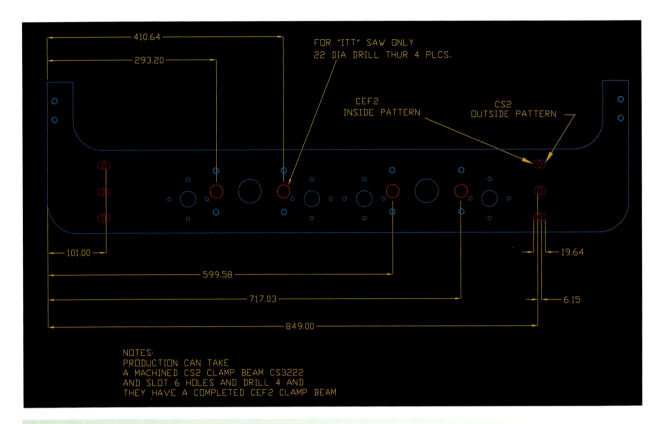

Clamp beam machining

MetlSaw Systems, Inc.

Patricia O'Brien Landscape Architecture (POBLA)

Patricia O'Brien Landscape Architecture has been using AutoCAD for eight years. Because of the nature of the profession, her firm usually works with a composite of several CAD drawings, each of which may come from a different professional organization involved with the same project.

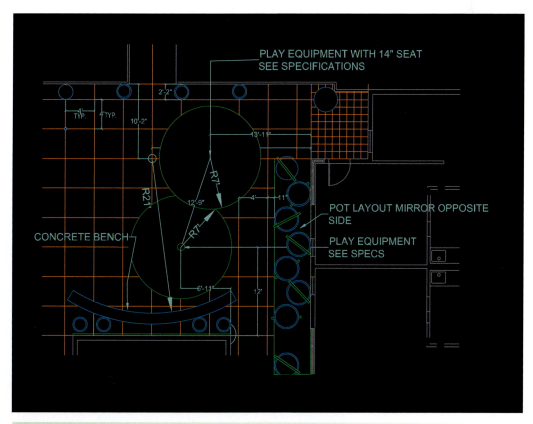

This is an example of the layout of an urban daycare recreation area.

Patricia O'Brien Landscape Architecture

The following three drawings are details that accompany a site design.

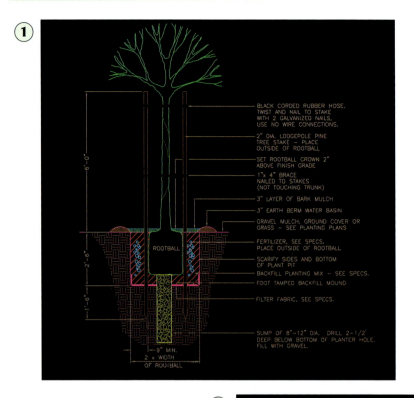

1

BLACK CORDED RUBBER HOSE.
TWIST AND NAIL TO STAKE
WITH 2 GALVANIZED NAILS,
USE NO WIRE CONNECTIONS.

2" DIA. LODGEPOLE PINE
TREE STAKE – PLACE
OUTSIDE OF ROOTBALL

SET ROOTBALL CROWN 2"
ABOVE FINISH GRADE

1" x 4" BRACE
NAILED TO STAKES
(NOT TOUCHING TRUNK)

3" LAYER OF BARK MULCH

3" EARTH BERM WATER BASIN

GRAVEL MULCH, GROUND COVER OR
GRASS – SEE PLANTING PLANS

FERTILIZER, SEE SPECS.
PLACE OUTSIDE OF ROOTBALL

SCARIFY SIDES AND BOTTOM
OF PLANT PIT

BACKFILL PLANTING MIX – SEE SPECS.

FOOT TAMPED BACKFILL MOUND

FILTER FABRIC, SEE SPECS.

SUMP OF 8"–12" DIA. DRILL 2-1/2'
DEEP BELOW BOTTOM OF PLANTER HOLE.
FILL WITH GRAVEL.

6'-0"

2'-6"

1'-6"

ROOTBALL

9" MIN.
2 x WIDTH
OF ROOTBALL

2

REMOVE NURSERY STAKE
AND ATTACH TO WALL WITH
VINE TIES–SEE SPECS.
MIN. 5 TIES PER PLANT

SCREEN WALL, SEE ARCH. DWGS.

PLANTING BACKFILL – SEE SPECS

GRAVEL MULCH

FINISH GRADE

2 x ROOTBALL

6"

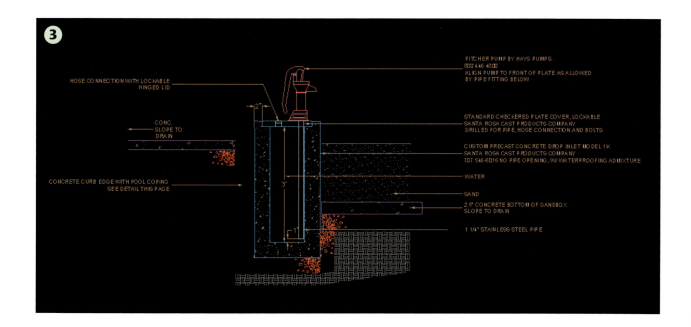

3

HOSE CONNECTION WITH LOCKABLE HINGED LID

CONC. SLOPE TO DRAIN

CONCRETE CURB EDGE WITH POOL COPING SEE DETAIL THIS PAGE

PITCHER PUMP BY HAYS PUMPS 800 465 4800 ALIGN PUMP TO FRONT OF PLATE AS ALLOWED BY PIPE FITTING BELOW

STANDARD CHECKERED PLATE COVER, LOCKABLE SANTA ROSA CAST PRODUCTS COMPANY DRILLED FOR PIPE, HOSE CONNECTION AND BOLTS

CUSTOM PRECAST CONCRETE DROP INLET MODEL 1K SANTA ROSA CAST PRODUCTS COMPANY 707 545-6016 NO PIPE OPENING, W/ WATERPROOFING ADMIXTURE

WATER

SAND

2.5" CONCRETE BOTTOM OF SANDBOX SLOPE TO DRAIN

1 1/4" STAINLESS STEEL PIPE

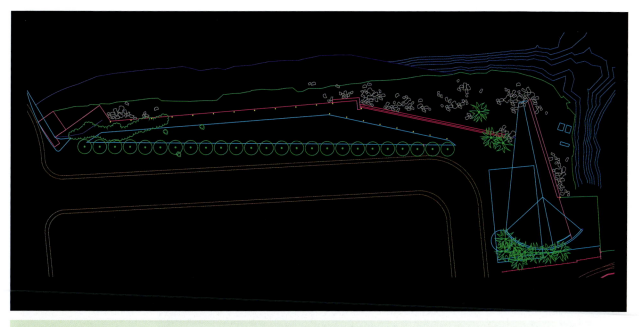

The last sample from POBLA is the design for a small park in San Francisco at a rocky section of the Bay coastline.

Patricia O'Brien Landscape Architecture

Kappe Architects

Ron Kappe designs residential and commercial projects. His firm uses AutoCAD for their design and construction drawings.

This sample is a special wood French window detail.

This sample is a site plan for a city's corporate industrial yard, including light industrial shops, a garage, and administrative offices.

Kappe Architects

The following drawings are an elevation, two sections, and a roof detail from a residential design.

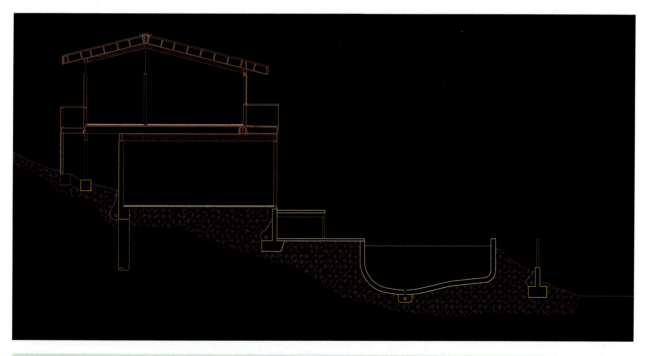

Section through bedroom and swimming pool

Kappe Architects

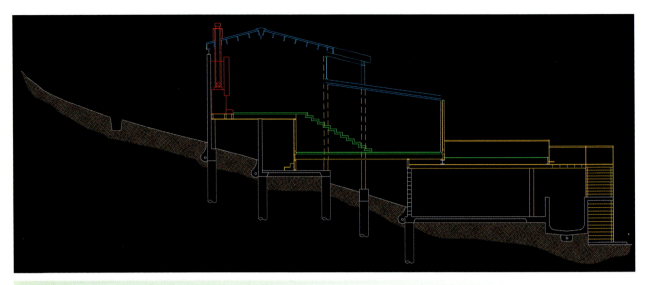

Section through great room, entry, and lap pool

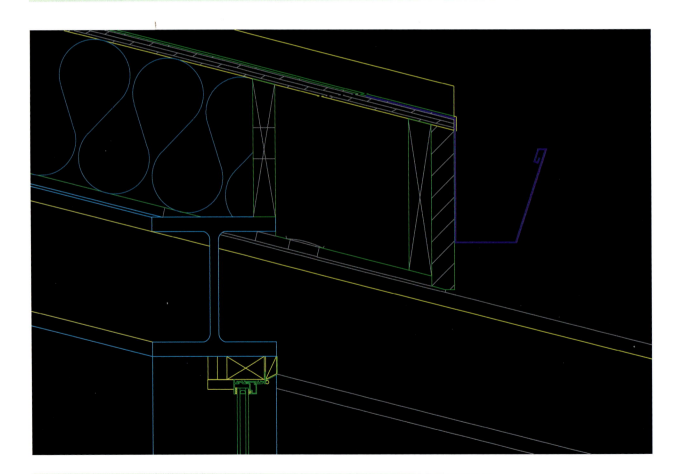

Detail of metal roof overhang

Tip

Copy is an option for each of the five commands that work with grips, allowing you to copy while moving, rotating, etc. Because of these options, you can copy lines with grips in ways that you cannot do with just the Copy command by itself.

Summary

This chapter has been an introduction to the basic selection tools and a discussion of the three methods of selecting lines. Understanding the selecting process and the selection tools that are at your disposal will help you a great deal in gaining a good working knowledge of AutoCAD.

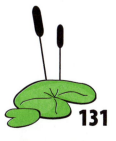

Chapter 9

Controlling the View of Your Drawing

As you work on your drawing, you will adjust your view often. Sometimes you will need to enlarge the view to do detailed work in a small area. Then you may want to work in another small area on the other side of the sheet. At other times you will want to see the entire drawing on the screen. This chapter introduces the tools that AutoCAD provides to manipulate the view of your drawing. You will learn:

- How to use a window to enlarge a portion of the drawing

- How to enlarge or shrink your drawing on the fly

- Several other tools for controlling the size of your drawing

- Two ways to slide your drawing around in the drawing area

Adjusting the Magnification

Magnification

The size of a drawing in the drawing area. Changing the magnification does not change the size of lines or other items in the drawing, just your view of them.

To work effectively on your drawing, you need to be able to adjust the **magnification** of the lines and other items, and the *Zooming* tools allow you to do this. Each **zoom option** gives you a unique way of adjusting the magnification of your drawing. We will look at a few of the most popular ones. As you work with the zooming tools, note that you are changing only the view, not the actual size of items in the drawing.

Zoom option

Any of several possible ways to change the magnification of the drawing in the drawing area. Zoom options are all part of the Zoom command.

Using a Window to Zoom in Closer

When you display your entire drawing on the screen, the details are usually too small to be seen clearly. If this is the case, you can use the Zoom Window option to enlarge a particular area and make the drawing appear closer.

1. On the Standard toolbar, click the Zoom Window icon.

The Zoom window is formed by picking two points that serve as opposite corners of a rectangle. Everything in the rectangle will be shown in the drawing area.

2. In your drawing, pick a point near the area you wish to enlarge. As you move the cursor away from that point, you start forming a window.

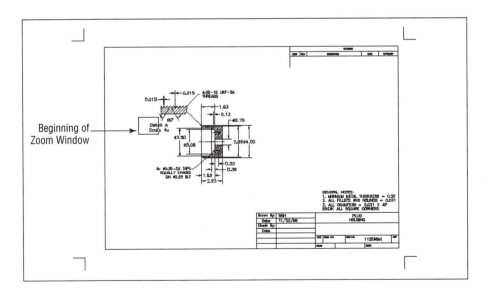

Beginning of Zoom Window

3. Drag to create a window until it surrounds the area that you wish to enlarge.

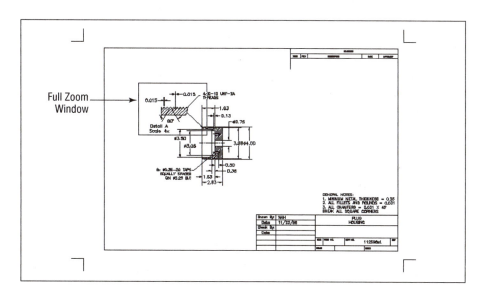

4. Click to establish the other corner of the window. The area inside the window is enlarged and fills the drawing area.

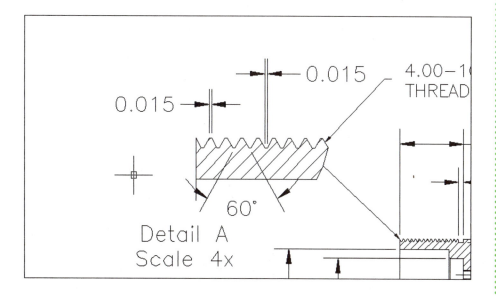

135

Recalling the Previous Magnification

After using any Zoom option, you can go back to the previous **view** of your drawing by using the Zoom Previous option.

1. In the previous operation, we zoomed into a small area of a drawing. Now click the Zoom Previous icon on the Standard toolbar (next to the Zoom Window icon).

2. The previous view of the full drawing is recalled.

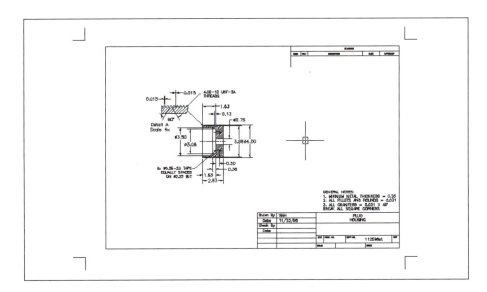

View
The part of your drawing that is currently visible in the drawing area. It may be the whole drawing or an enlarged portion of it.

Zoom Previous can be used repeatedly to "undo" the last few zooms.

Zoom in
To increase the magnification of a drawing so that items in the drawing appear bigger, and the drawing seems to be closer.

Zoom out
To decrease the magnification of a drawing so that items in the drawing appear smaller. And the drawing seems to be further away.

Tip

Many times it's convenient to use Zoom Window to **zoom in** on an area, work on that area, and then use Zoom Previous to **zoom out** to where you were before. After that, you can use Zoom Window again to zoom in on a different area, and so on.

Zooming to a Percentage of the Current Magnification

When you are working on your drawing and want to make a slight adjustment to the magnification, you can use the Zoom Scale option. It allows you to magnify or shrink the current view by a percentage of its current size.

1. If you start with a full view of your drawing, it will come close to filling the drawing area.

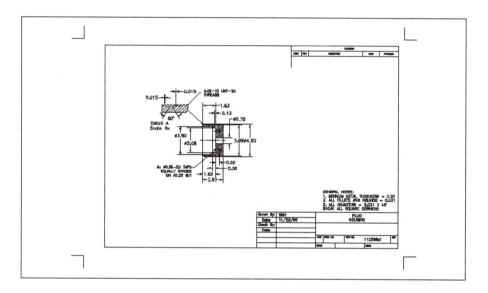

2. Open the Zoom flyout on the Standard toolbar and click the Zoom Scale icon.

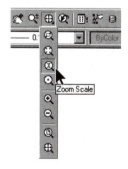

3. Type in the percentage you wish, in decimal form, followed by an *x*, and then press ↵. (I will use **.6x** in the example.)

4. The view will change by the percentage you entered. (In the example, the drawing in the new view was shrunk to 60% of its size in the previous view.)

To zoom out to 80%, you would enter **.8x**. To zoom in to 125%, you would enter **1.25x**. The *x* tells AutoCAD to zoom relative to the current view.

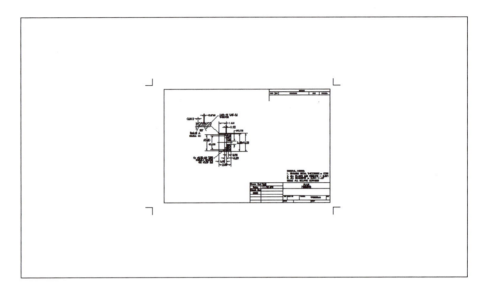

> **Tip**
>
> Also on the Zoom flyout are the "Zoom +" and "Zoom −" options. They work like Zoom Scale but are preset to Zoom to 150% (zooming in) and to 50% (zooming out), respectively.

Zooming in Realtime Mode

When you need to zoom in or zoom out, there is a quick way to do this **dynamically**. The view will change as you drag the mouse.

Dynamically
Performed in such a way that the changes appear on the screen as you are making them (in "real time"), rather than after you have finished a command.

1. Click the Zoom Realtime icon on the Standard toolbar.

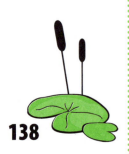

2. When you move the cursor onto the drawing, the crosshairs will change to an icon similar to the Zoom Realtime button.

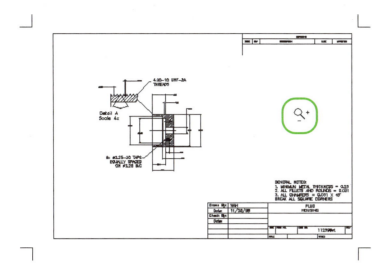

The Zoom Realtime cursor shows a magnifying glass with a plus on one side of the handle and a minus on the other.

3. Hold down the left mouse button and drag the cursor down to zoom out or up to zoom in.

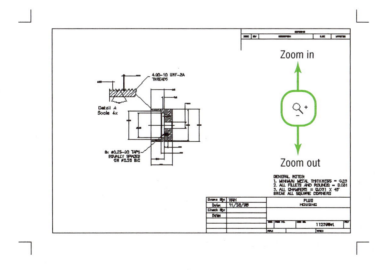

With the Zoom Realtime option, moving the cursor to the right or left has no effect. It's the up and down motion that controls the change in magnification of the view.

4. When the drawing is the right size for you, release the mouse button.

5. Repeat steps 3 and 4 if you need to fine-tune the view.

6. When you have the view you want, press the Esc key to cancel Zoom Realtime.

Zoom Realtime keeps running until you cancel it by pressing the Esc or Enter keys.

Zooming to the Drawing Extents

After you have been zooming in and out and working on your drawing in several different views, you will eventually need to view your drawing in full. The quickest and easiest way to get that full view is to use the Zoom Extents option. This option will change the magnification of the view in such a way that everything you have drawn will be displayed and fill the screen. This view of the drawing is called the **drawing extents**.

Drawing extents

A rectangle that is just large enough to contain all visible items in the current drawing. The drawing extents rectangle will change in size and shape as lines are added or deleted at the outer edges of the drawing.

1. If you have zoomed in, parts of your drawing will be off the drawing area.

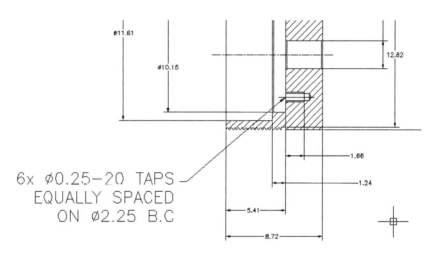

2. Open the Zoom flyout on the Standard toolbar and click on the Zoom Extents icon.

3. The view will change to display all visible lines in the drawing, and to fill the drawing area with them.

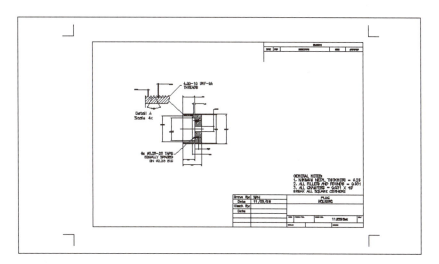

When zoomed to extents, extremities of the drawing will extend almost to the edge of the drawing area.

See Also The Drawing Extents of a drawing include all *visible* items in the drawing, when all layers are turned on. To learn how to control the visibility of lines, see Chapter 11: "Working with Layers and Properties."

Other Zooming Tools

There are more zooming options than we have room to cover in this book, but you should take a look at them all. An easy way to access all the zooming tools is by using the keyboard.

1. When you type **z** ↵, the Zoom command starts and most zoom options are shown in the Command window.

2. For the next step, you have several choices. You can:

⬧ Start a zoom window

⬧ Enter a zoom scale

- ◆ Press ↵ to start Zoom Realtime

- ◆ Type in the first letter of any option listed within the brackets [ ] and then press ↵ to start that option.

This has been a presentation of some of the most often-used Zoom options. In the next section, we look at another view control tool: the Pan options.

Panning

Panning

The process of sliding the current drawing around on the drawing area without changing the magnification of the view.

Once you have zoomed to the appropriate magnification of your drawing (see the previous section), use the Pan tools to slide your drawing around while maintaining that magnification. **Panning** is comparable to using the optional slide bars that, when enabled, sit on the right side and bottom of the drawing area. We will look at two of AutoCAD's panning tools: Realtime Pan and Panning with Points.

Panning in Realtime Mode

Pan Realtime is similar to Zoom Realtime, discussed in the previous section. The view changes dynamically as you move the cursor.

1. When you work on a section of the drawing, zoom in to increase the magnification.

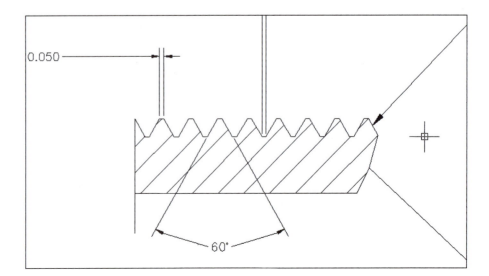

2. To move from one section of the drawing to another, without changing the magnification, pick the Pan Realtime icon on the Standard toolbar.

3. When you move the cursor back onto the drawing area, the crosshair will change to an icon of a hand, similar to the Pan Realtime button.

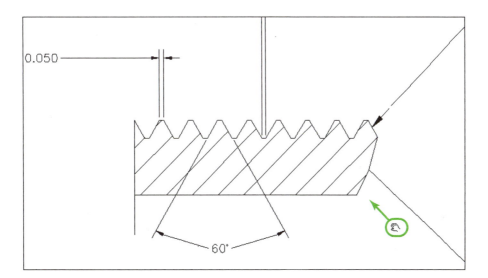

Pan Realtime uses a cursor that looks like a hand that might slide a drawing around on a table. It's similar to the Pan Realtime button on the Standard toolbar.

4. Hold down the left mouse button as you move the Pan Realtime cursor across the drawing area. The drawing moves with the cursor.

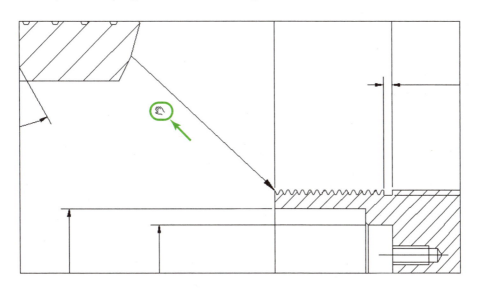

When using Pan Realtime, you can move the cursor in any direction.

5. When you have panned to the section of the drawing that you want to work on next, release the mouse button.

6. Repeat steps 4 and 5 to pan further across the drawing, or to fine-tune your view.

7. When you have the view you want, press the Esc key to cancel Pan Realtime.

Pan Realtime keeps running until you cancel it, by pressing the Esc or Enter key.

Tip

If you right-click while using Realtime Pan or Realtime Zoom, a shortcut menu appears that has several options, including one for switching between Pan and Zoom Realtime, and one to cancel whichever one is current. Almost all the options are very useful. Experiment.

Using Two Points to Pan

You can use the Pan Point command to pan your drawing a specified distance and direction. If, for example, you wanted to move your drawing to the right so that a line that is currently in the middle of the drawing area would then be near the right side of the drawing area, you would use Pan Point as shown below.

Pan Point allows you to be very precise in making a pan, but it does not perform dynamically, as does Pan Realtime.

1. Type **–p** ↵.

2. Pick a point near the line that you intend to move to the right side of the drawing area.

Pan Point can also be started by clicking View ➤ Pan ➤ Point on the pull-down menus.

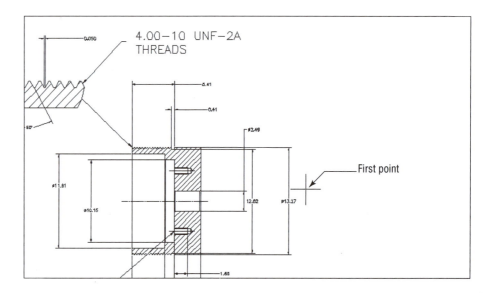

3. Pick a second point near the right side of the drawing area.

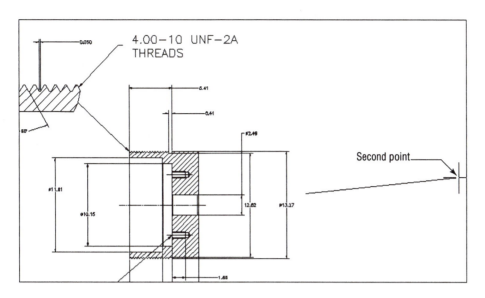

4. The drawing is moved to the right.

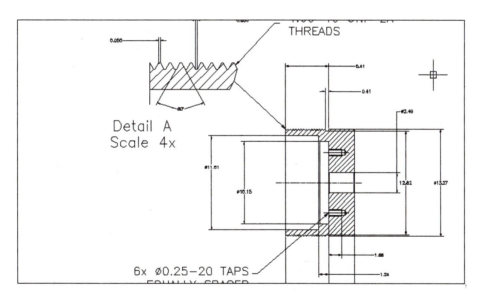

Tip

Almost all of the Panning and Zooming options can be used while another command is running. This is called using a command **transparently**.

Pan Point can be used to pan your drawing in any direction.

Pan Point is a good substitute for Pan Realtime if your drawing is very complex and if your graphics card is not very powerful.

Transparently
Performed while another command is currently in progress without causing the current command to be canceled. When commands are run transparently, they temporarily interrupt the current command.

Summary

The most important zooming and panning options have been presented in this chapter. If you have an Intellimouse (the one with a wheel between the two buttons) you can also use the wheel in various ways to Realtime Pan and Zoom.

Chapter 10

Correcting Errors

In computer drafting, as in manual drafting, there will be changes and revisions to be made to most drawings. That's all part of the work. But there are also the errors that we make while using AutoCAD, and for these we need specific tools to correct. In this chapter, we will look at some of the common errors made by AutoCAD users and the tools provided for correcting them. Below is a list of the essential skills you will learn in Chapter 10.

- Undoing the effect of a command

- Undoing part of the effect of a command

- Canceling a command

- Getting rid of unwanted windows and squares

- Getting help from AutoCAD

Fixing Mistakes

When you have used a command and ended it, and then realize that the results are wrong, you need to reverse what you have done. AutoCAD offers several tools to help you do this. One of them is similar to the Undo command that you may have used in other Windows applications.

The U Command

In AutoCAD, the basic command for undoing things is the U command. Auto-CAD also offers an Undo command, which is different and is discussed below.

1. As an example, let's say you have used the Offset command twice to create vertical lines in the diagram below and then ended the command. Now you realize that the first offset distance was wrong.

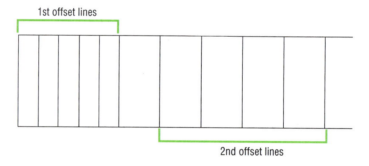

1st offset lines

2nd offset lines

The Undo button starts the U command in AutoCAD. It does the same thing as the Undo command in other Windows programs.

2. To correct the error, you will need to undo the last two commands and start again. Move the cursor to the Undo button on the Standard toolbar.

Each time you use the U command, everything done in one use of a command is undone.

3. Click once. The last set of offset lines is deleted.

4. Click again. The first set of offset lines is deleted.

Tip

If you use the U command too many times and undo too much, you can use the Redo command (its button is the right of the Undo button) to undo the last undo, but only the last one.

The U command can also be started by typing **u** ↵. Then you can press ↵ to restart the command and keep undoing.

The Undo Command

The Undo command is unique to AutoCAD and can be started only through the keyboard. It is more powerful than the U command, and has several options. Be careful how you use it.

1. Type **undo** ↵, then look at the Command window.

```
Select objects:
Command: undo
Enter the number of operations to undo or [Auto/Control/BEgin/End/Mark/Back] <1>:
```

In AutoCAD, the Undo command is a special, complex command. The U command is like the Undo command in other programs.

2. You have several options, including one that allows you to enter the number of steps you would like to undo. Below is a list of the options:

Auto: Controls whether the Undo command undoes macros as a single command or as several commands.

Control: Determines whether the Undo and U commands are disabled, and whether the Undo command can undo more than one command at a time.

Begin, End: When used, Begin marks a point in the command sequence after which all commands will be undone together when End is entered.

Mark: Marks a point in the command sequence to be used with Back.

Back: Undoes all previous commands back to where Mark was used. If Mark is not used, undoes everything back to the last time the drawing was saved. If drawing has not been saved, undoes all work done on the drawing since the beginning of the drawing session.

Number: Allows you to enter the number of previously used commands to undo.

Warning

Be careful when using the Undo command. If you use the Back option, AutoCAD may undo everything you've done since your last Save. Stick with the U command (Undo icon on the Standard toolbar) until you are certain how to use the Undo command.

Undoing in the Middle of a Command

Some commands have Undo as an option while the command is running. This allows you to correct an error without stopping the command. In our example, we'll use the Trim command.

1. Once the Trim command is started, the cutting edges are selected first.

Cutting edge

2. As you trim lines, you may accidentally trim a line that you didn't intend to trim.

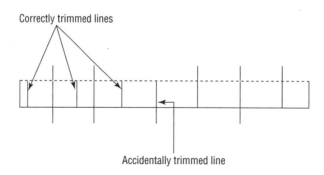

Correctly trimmed lines

Accidentally trimmed line

If a command has an Undo option, you can use the U command while in the middle of executing the command. Trim, Extend, Line, and Polyline are commands that have this option.

3. Type **u** ↵. The last line that was trimmed is restored.

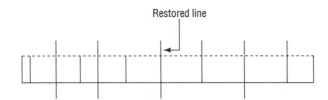

Restored line

4. Continue trimming the proper lines to trim. Press ↵ when finished.

The three tools described above should enable you to correct most drawing mistakes that you make in the course of using AutoCAD.

Getting Out of Trouble: The Esc Key

Beginning AutoCAD users often make procedural mistakes while using a command. They do something wrong or get stuck. Here are some examples of trouble you might get into, and ways to get out.

Canceling a Command Mid-Stream

You may get confused or lost in the middle of a command's operation, and can't figure out what to do next. Rather than get frustrated, you can cancel the command and try again.

1. When a command is running, lines may be selected and you may (for example) be prompted for a base point or displacement.

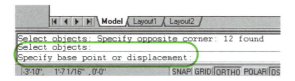

```
Select objects: Specify opposite corner: 12 found
Select objects:
Specify base point or displacement:
-3'-10", 1'-7 1/16" , 0'-0"          SNAP GRID ORTHO POLAR OS
```

2. If you don't know what to pick as a base point or what to enter as a displacement, you can cancel the command at this point to rethink what you are doing. Press the Esc key to cancel the command.

Getting Rid of Unwanted Grips

Grips can appear on lines in ways that can confuse the beginner. For example, suppose you make the mistake of picking a line before starting a command when you intended to start the command first. The line will ghost, and grips will appear on it. This may be confusing if you don't know what to do next, but the Esc key will help you out here.

1. Any time a line is picked without a command running, the line will **ghost** and **grips** will appear at the midpoint and endpoints of the line.

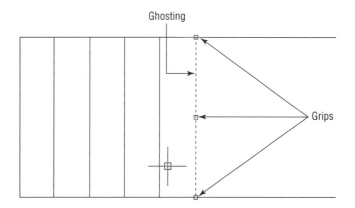

Ghosting

Grips

2. Press the Esc key twice to remove the ghosting and the grips.

3. Select the next command to use and continue working.

See Also AutoCAD allows lines to be selected with no command running because this is one way of using several of the Modify commands. See Chapter 8: "Selecting Lines and Other Items in Your Drawing."

If you use the Esc key to cancel the Line command after drawing a few segments, AutoCAD will retain those first segments, up to the last point picked.

Ghosting

The process of a line temporarily changing into one made up of small dashes. This change indicates that the line has been selected.

Grips

Small, colored squares that appear on lines that have been selected when no command is running. They are a tool for quickly modifying lines.

When you press the Esc key twice, the first keystroke ends the ghosting of the line, and the second removes the grips.

Getting Rid of Unwanted Selection Windows

There are a couple of situations in which you may find your cursor dragging open a window that you didn't intend to create, and you won't know why Auto-CAD is doing this. What you're seeing is a selection feature called **implied windowing**, and it works like this:

 ◇ If you are prompted to Select objects and you try to pick a line but miss it and instead pick a blank space, a selection window is started.

 ◇ And, when no command is running, if you pick a point in a blank portion of the drawing area, a selection window is also started.

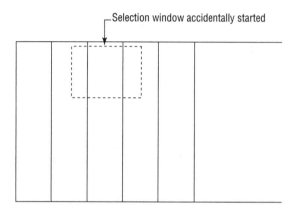

Selection window accidentally started

See Also Selection windows are made of solid lines if they are regular and dashed lines if they are crossing windows. See Chapter 8: "Selecting Lines and Other Items in your Drawing."

1. In either situation there are two ways out of this trouble:

 ◇ You can press the Esc key to cancel the window

 ◇ You can pick another point to complete the window, making sure that your window selects nothing.

2. After the window is gone, you can continue with the selection process, or start a command.

This section has brought up some of the common ways that new users get into trouble, and illustrated how the Esc key can get them out of it.

Implied Windowing
A process by which a selection window is started by picking a point in a blank portion of the drawing area, when the Select Objects prompt is active or when no commands are running.

Tip

In the Selection tab of the Options dialog box, you can disable grips, prevent the ghosting of lines that are accidentally selected when no command is running (turn off Noun/Verb Selection), and prevent selection windows from starting up accidentally (turn off Implied Windowing).

Using the Help Feature

Like most full-featured software, AutoCAD offers help in understanding its commands. We will look at two of the most basic ways that help is available in the program.

General Help

When you want to learn about a command using the AutoCAD Help feature, one of your options is to look up the command in the on-screen Index.

1. With no command running, click Help ➢ AutoCAD Help on the pull-down menus.

2. In the Help Topics: AutoCAD Help dialog box, be sure the Index tab is active.

Through the Help Topics: AutoCAD Help dialog box, you can also access the Contents tab, which has electronic versions of the AutoCAD 2000 manuals.

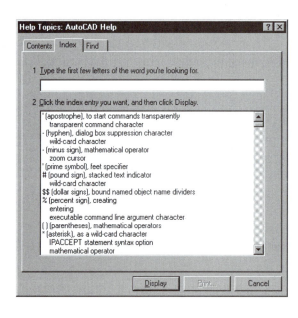

3. Type in the name of the command you wish to look up. As you type the letters, the list below automatically scrolls to the place where the command should be found.

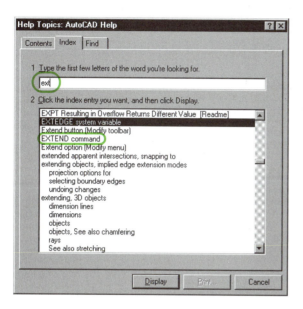

4. When you see the command in the list, click on it to highlight it, then click the Display button at the bottom of the dialog box. (In the example, you would highlight "EXTEND command" in the list.)

5. If more than one topic fits the command name, the Topics Found dialog box displays the list of topics that were found.

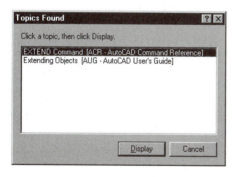

Through the AutoCAD Command Reference window, you can access an electronic version of the Glossary that's in the User's Guide. Click the Glossary button near the top of the window.

6. Highlight the topic of your choice and click the Display button. The AutoCAD Command Reference window opens to a discussion of the command you chose.

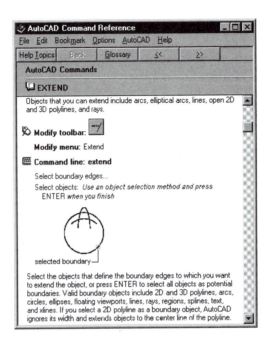

Tip

Although this approach to getting help requires several steps, it offers you a list of related topics and allows you to do some browsing.

Specific Help for the Current Command

Context-sensitive help

A process in the Help feature whereby information about a command is displayed while that command is running.

If you have started a command but get confused about how to complete it, you can get immediate help for that command. This is called **context-sensitive help**.

1. Once a command has been started, the Command window displays prompts for working through the steps of that command.

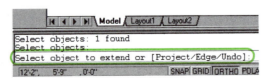

2. Press the F1 key at any time. The AutoCAD Command Reference window opens to a discussion of the command that is running.

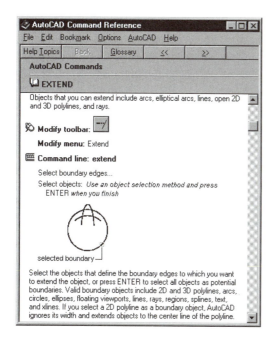

The AutoCAD Command reference window will often contain some words you can click for further information. These hyperlink words appear in a different color from the regular text, and the cursor changes to a hand with the index finger pointing when it's over them.

Tip

Context-sensitive help is faster than using the Index, but you don't get to browse the list of topics.

Summary

This chapter has included several tools for correcting errors in drawing, as well as some mistakes in executing commands that beginners often make. We also looked briefly at a couple of the Help features that come with AutoCAD.

Part 3

Additional AutoCAD Features for the Beginner

As you build up your skills in creating AutoCAD drawings, you will find the features introduced in the following chapters to be quite useful. The elements of the program to be covered here are what makes using CAD so different from manual drafting. Chapter 11 delves into the subject of layers and properties. In Chapter 12, you'll see how to use and modify text in a drawing. Following that, I introduce the basics of dimensioning in Chapter 13. The very useful feature of grouping lines into what AutoCAD calls "blocks" is discussed in Chapter 14. Because you will usually have to get everything in your drawing onto a piece of paper, the book ends with Chapter 15, where we look at the process of printing and plotting.

Additional AutoCAD Features for the Beginner

Chapter 11

Working with Layers and Properties

The lines and other items in your drawings are on layers. Every AutoCAD drawing has at least one layer, the default layer 0, which has the various default properties discussed in other chapters, but you can define your own layers and assign properties to them. As your work in AutoCAD becomes more complex, you may want to use this feature to organize the elements of a drawing. Placing different types of objects or information on separate layers allows you to assign and modify the properties of those objects—such as color or visibility—one layer at a time. In this chapter, we'll look at how to set up and use layers, and how to work with some of AutoCAD's properties.

Layers

Layers are the electronic version of the now obsolete overlays that were once used with registration points in manual drafting. Three or four sheets, each containing different kinds of information, were laid atop one another. The bottom one was usually a base drawing, like a floor plan or a site plan. Subsequent sheets were placed on top and additional information, such as an electrical layout, was drawn on them. The registration points kept the sheets aligned, and, when stacked together, the sheets made up a whole drawing. Layers work like this, too, but they are far more powerful. While a manual drafter was limited to a maximum of about six overlays, there is no limit to the number of layers an AutoCAD user can have. They are a tool for organizing your drawing and controlling the visibility and other **properties** of the drawing's lines.

Creating a New Layer and Assigning It a Color

When you start up a new drawing, it has one layer—the 0 (zero) layer—and everything you draw is on that layer. Once your drawing takes on some complexity, setting up new layers will help organize the parts of your drawing.

1. Click the Layers button on the Object Properties toolbar to bring up the Layer Properties Manager dialog box.

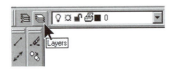

2. Click the New button. A new layer, called Layer1, will appear in the list. It will be highlighted.

Layers

Divisions in a drawing that act like transparent drafting sheets that are laid on top of each other. Some lines are on one sheet, and others are on other sheets. When you look through all of them, you see your entire drawing.

Properties

Characteristics of lines or of layers that have lines on them. Color is a property that can be assigned to a line or a layer. When assigned to a layer, all lines on that layer have that assigned property.

The Layer Properties Manager dialog box has a minimum size, but you can make it as big as the screen will allow.

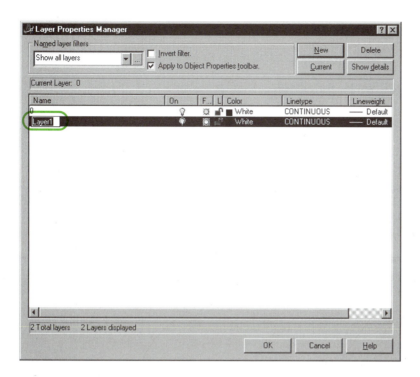

All AutoCAD drawings have a 0 layer (read "zero layer") that cannot be deleted or renamed.

3. Type in the name of the new layer that you prefer—for example, **Walls**—and press ↵.

AutoCAD 2000 will retain the uppercase and lowercase characters that you use for layer names.

Tip

Layer names usually represent specific types of things that the objects in your drawing represent, like doors, dimensions, trees, hidden lines, centerlines, etc. In complex layer-naming systems, names sometimes follow a layer standard, such as ST-W-E for Structural-Wall- Existing.

4. Click the square color swatch for the new layer in the Color column.

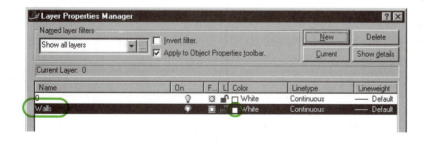

The first seven of the Standard colors have names and numbers, while the rest of the 256 colors available have only numbers.

5. This brings up the Select Color dialog box. The Standard Colors are on a row at the top.

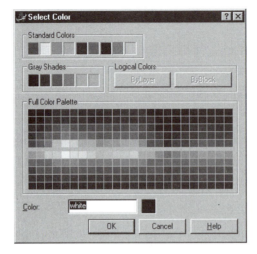

 Tip

Many AutoCAD users start by using the row of Standard Colors for layers, then go to the Gray Shades and the Full Color Palette if necessary.

6. Click a color of your choice for the layer, and then click OK to return to the Layer Properties Manager.

7. Repeat steps 2 through 6 for each additional new layer you wish to create.

8. Click the OK button at the bottom of the dialog box to return to your drawing.

See Also When new layers are created, the lines in your drawing are still on the 0 layer and will have to be moved to the new layers. Skip to the section titled *Assigning Items in the Drawing to a New Layer,* later in this chapter, to see how to do this.

Drawing Lines on a Particular Layer

Once layers have been set up, you can choose a layer to be the **current layer**. Any new lines drawn will be drawn on the current layer. To make a layer the current layer, follow these steps:

1. Click the Layer control on the Object Properties toolbar.

Layer control

2. Locate the layer you wish to make current—scroll if necessary—and click directly on that layer's name.

Warning

When making a layer current, be sure to click the layer's name rather than one of the icons to the left of the name. Otherwise, you might change some other property of the layer.

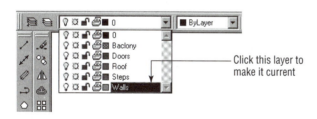

Click this layer to make it current

3. The layer you chose is now displayed in the Layer control. All new lines that are drawn subsequently will be on the new current layer.

Current layer
The active layer. All lines that are drawn while a layer is the current layer will be on that layer.

The Layer control is a drop-down list of the defined layers in the drawing, with the current layer (in the illustration, the default layer 0) displayed when the drop-down is closed. When you click on the current layer, the list of layers opens up.

Once layers have been set up, they will be displayed in numerical and alphabetical order, with the numerical ones first.

Making a Layer Invisible

At times you will want all lines on a layer to be invisible. To do this you can freeze a layer or turn it off. All lines on a layer that has been frozen or turned off become invisible until you "thaw" the layer or turn it on again. The differences between freezing a layer and turning it off are technical and beyond the scope of this book, but the procedure is the same. So I will illustrate the procedure for freezing and thawing a layer. Once you've learned that, you can easily apply it to turning layers off and on.

Making lines invisible is different than erasing lines. In freezing a layer (or in turning a layer off), we make the lines temporarily invisible because we don't need them right now, or they are in the way. We will recall them later.

The four icons next to a layer's name and color swatch are a light bulb, sun, lock, and printer. They are all on/off toggles that can be changed in this list. The light bulb is the toggle for turning layers off and on and the sun is for freeze/thaw; the other two icons are the lock/unlock and print/no print toggles. To change a color or create a new layer, you have to click the Layer button and open the Layer Properties Manager dialog box.

1. In the floor plan below, we want to make the door lines invisible.

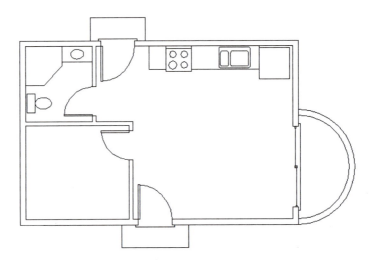

2. Open the Layer control drop-down list. Notice that each layer has a row of icons to the left of its name.

3. To freeze a layer, click that layer's sun icon.

4. The sun icon turns into a snowflake icon.

5. Click the layer at the top of the list to keep it as the current layer, close the list, and return to your drawing. Lines on the frozen layer will now be invisible.

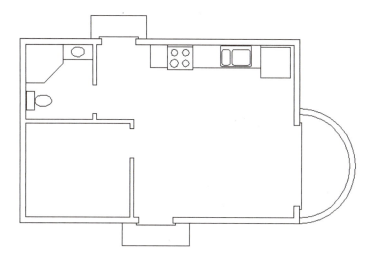

6. To make the frozen layer visible again (that is, to "thaw" it), follow the same procedure but click the snowflake to change it back into a sun.

Warning

The current layer can be turned off, but it cannot be frozen. To freeze that layer, you must first make another layer current, and then freeze the layer that had been previously current.

To make a layer that's been turned off visible again (that is, to turn it back on), click the darkened light bulb to light it up again.

Changing the Properties of Objects

Once you have set up new layers, there will usually be lines and other objects in your drawing that you need to move from one layer to another. There will also be times when you will need to find out what layer an item is on. This section illustrates how to accomplish these tasks.

Assigning Items in the Drawing to a New Layer

You can use the Properties window to move an item from one layer to another.

1. Select the line(s) in your drawing that will be moved to a different layer.

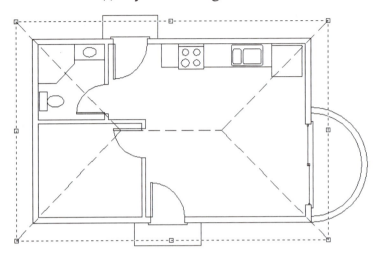

When lines are selected and no command is running, the lines ghost and grips appear on them. See Chapter 8: "Selecting Lines and Other Items in Your Drawing."

2. Click the Properties button on the Standard toolbar.

After making a selection, you can right-click and select Properties from the shortcut menu that appears, to bring up the Properties window.

3. In the Properties window, click Layer in the left column.

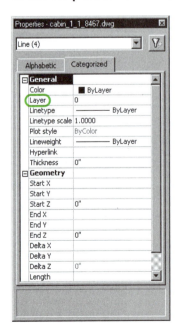

168

4. In the right column, click the down-arrow in the Layer row to open the drop-down list, and then click the layer to which you wish to move the selected lines.

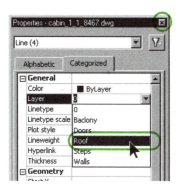

5. Click the X in the upper-right corner of the Properties window to close it.

6. Press the Esc key twice to remove the grips.

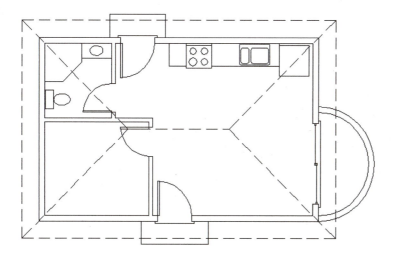

The Properties window can be docked on the left or right side of the drawing area. When docked, it takes up space on the screen, but it doesn't obscure part of your drawing. (You can resize the docked window horizontally by dragging its right or left border.)

Getting Information About an Item in the Drawing

When you are working with existing lines in your drawing, you may want to get information about those lines, such as what layer they are on.

1. Select the lines or items in your drawing about which you need information.

2. Open the Inquiry flyout by clicking and holding down the Distance button on the Standard toolbar.

3. With the Inquiry flyout displayed, continue holding the mouse button down, and slide the cursor down the flyout toolbar to the List icon. Then release the mouse button.

4. The Text Screen appears with information about the selected objects. For the arc selected in this example, we see the layer it's on, as well as the location of its center point, its radius, and related information. In general, whatever characteristics define the object will be listed here.

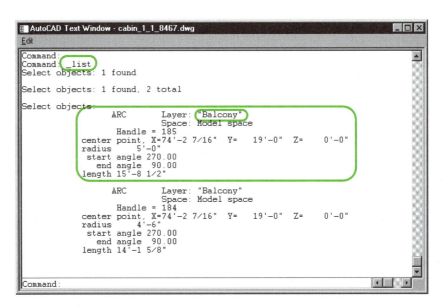

5. When finished, press the F2 key to return to your drawing, or close the window by clicking the X in the upper-right corner.

Changing the Current Layer

Each new line or other object you draw is added to the current layer. Suppose you need to draw something on a particular layer that is not current, such as the Doors or Roof layer in our example. To do this, you will need to make that layer the current layer. AutoCAD offers a quick and easy way to change the current layer.

1. Click the Make Object's Layer Current icon on the Object Properties toolbar.

2. Click on a line that is on the layer you want to make current. That layer now becomes the current layer.

Once a layer is current, all lines drawn after that will be on that layer.

Applying the Properties of One Line to Another Line

When you've defined properties for one line or other object and want to apply them to another object, you can use the quick-and-easy Match Properties tool. For example, suppose you've used the Offset command (Chapter 3) for offsetting a wall line to create a roof line. The new line has the same properties as the wall line, but you want it to be a roof line. You can use Match Properties to give the new line the properties that other roof lines have.

1. Click the Match Properties button on the Standard toolbar.

2. Click on a line whose properties you wish to transfer to another line.

3. Click on the line that you wish to take on the properties of the first line you selected. The line takes on those properties.

171

4. If necessary, continue to click on lines to match their properties to the first line selected.

5. When finished, press ↵.

Linetypes

Although you'll mostly use solid, continuous lines in your work, AutoCAD offers many other types of lines. A line's linetype is a property of the layer that line belongs to, and you control it through the Layer Properties Manager. When you need a dashed line or a dashdot line in your drawing, you can create a new layer for that line type and put those lines on their own layer. Linetypes have to be loaded into the current drawing, as a new drawing has only one linetype to start with: the continuous line.

Loading Linetypes and Assigning Them to Layers

You can load a **linetype** into a drawing when you are setting up layers, or at any time afterwards.

1. Click the Layer button on the Object Properties toolbar.

2. In the Layer Properties Manager dialog box, click the name of the linetype currently assigned to a layer you want to modify.

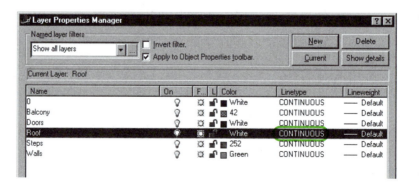

The Match Properties command will match many of the properties of a line to other selected lines, not just color and layer.

Linetype

A style of line, such as dashed, dashdot, continuous, center, etc. AutoCAD comes with 45 linetypes.

When a new layer is created, the linetype assigned to that layer will be Continuous if no layers are highlighted in the Layer Properties Manager dialog box. If a layer is highlighted, the new layer will take that layer's linetype.

3. In the Select Linetype dialog box, look for the line type you need. If it's in the list, go on to step 5. The linetype is already loaded in the drawing, and you just need to assign it to the layer. If the one you want isn't there, click the Load button.

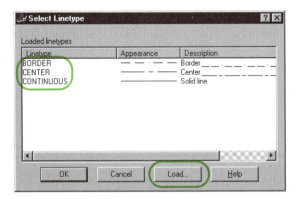

4. In the Load or Reload Linetypes dialog box, scroll down the list to the line type you want and click it to highlight it. Then click OK.

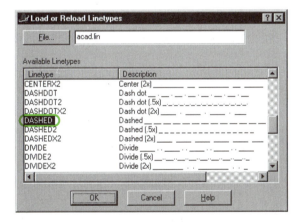

In the list of linetypes, the first 14 listed are in the International Standards Organization family and are used in metric drawings.

5. In the Select Linetype dialog box, click the newly loaded linetype to highlight it and click OK.

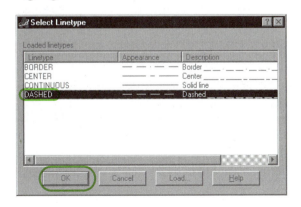

You can load several linetypes into your drawing at a time. Use the Ctrl key to highlight more than one line type in the Load or Reload Linetypes dialog box.

173

6. In the Layer Properties Manager, the highlighted layer now has the newly loaded linetype assigned to it. Click OK to return to your drawing.

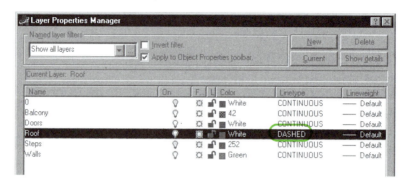

Adjusting the Linetype Scale Factor

For noncontinuous linetypes, the length of the dashes and the space between dashes are controlled by a Linetype Scale Factor setting. You will often need to adjust this setting to make the dashes be the right length for your drawing.

Larger linetype scale factors make the dashes longer and the spaces between dashes wider.

1. Type **ltscale** ↵. In the Command window, the current scale factor is displayed.

The number you use for the linetype scale factor is related to the scale at which the drawing will be printed. For example, the linetype scale factor for a drawing printed at a scale of 1/4" = 1'-0" will be 48; at a scale of 1/8" = 1'-0" the scale factor will be 96; at a scale of 1 m = 100 m it will be 100.

2. Type in the new scale factor and press ↵.

3. Check your drawing. If the dashes need further adjustment, repeat steps 1 and 2.

See Also   See Chapter 15 for more about scale factors.

Summary

The chapter has introduced you to the concepts of layers, and it has illustrated how properties such as colors and linetypes are assigned to layers. For a more thorough treatment of layers and properties, see *AutoCAD 2000: No Experience Required* by this author, or *Mastering AutoCAD 2000* by George Omura, both Sybex books.

Chapter 12

Putting Text into a Drawing

When you work with text in a drawing, you use skills in three areas: setting up a text style, putting text in the drawing, and modifying text that has already been placed in a drawing. AutoCAD has two kinds of text: single-line text and multiline text. They both use the same text styles, but you place them in the drawing differently and modify them using similar but somewhat different methods.

Text style
A named group of settings that control the appearance of text in your drawing.

Font
A collection of letters, characters, and punctuation marks that share common features of design and appearance.

You can certainly use the Standard text style as is, but the text font that it uses is quite primitive: all letters consist of only straight lines.

Setting Up a Text Style

A **text style** consists of a name for the style, a **font,** and various settings for the size and orientation of the text. Once you have several text styles to choose from, you use a style by making it current, or active.

Tip

If you need several sizes of the same font, does each one require a separate style? No. If you set up a text style so that the height of the text is set to 0, you can use the same text style to make text with various heights.

Creating a New Text Style

Each new AutoCAD drawing comes with a Standard text style. When you create a new text style, you make a copy of the Standard style and rename it, and then make any necessary changes to the aspects of the new style.

1. On the pull-down menus, click Format ➢ Text Style to bring up the Text Style dialog box.

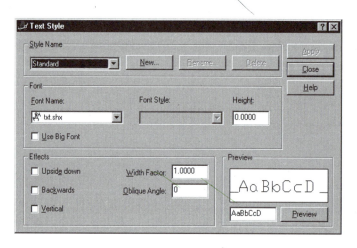

2. In the Style Name area, click the New button to bring up the New Text Style dialog box.

3. Enter a new text style name—you probably won't prefer to use the default "Style1" name—and click OK.

4. Back in the Text Style dialog box, the new text style name will replace Standard in the Style Name drop-down list. In the Font area, click in the Font Name drop-down list to open it.

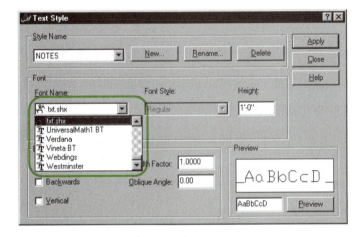

The Style Name drop-down list displays all the text styles that have been defined in the current drawing.

5. Scroll the list to find the font you wish to assign to this new text style, and click it to select it and to close the list.

6. For most AutoCAD text uses, you may also need to make changes to the following settings:

Font Style: for some fonts, you will have choices of bold, italic, and so on.

Height: Height of the uppercase characters.

Width Factor: A number greater than 1 gives you wider letters; less than 1, thinner.

Oblique Angle: Enter an angle to slant letters away from vertical.

When you select a font, its appearance is previewed in the Preview area of the Text Style dialog box. If you make changes to other text settings, they are also reflected in the Preview area.

If you leave the Height set to 0, you will be prompted for the text height when you place text in the drawing.

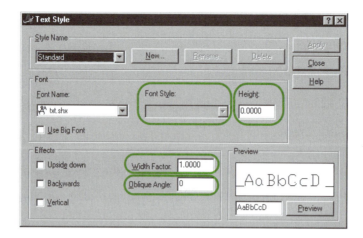

7. When you have made all your desired setting changes, click Apply to save the setting changes to the new text style. Then click Close.

Making an Existing Text Style Current

Current text style

The text style that is active in your drawing. New text put into a drawing is made in the current style.

When you follow the steps in the previous section to create a new text style, it becomes the **current text style**. New text you place in the drawing will be in that style. The Text Style dialog box can be used to change the current style from one text style to another.

1. Click Format ➢ Text Style to bring up the Text Style dialog box.

2. Click the drop-down list in the Style Name area to open it.

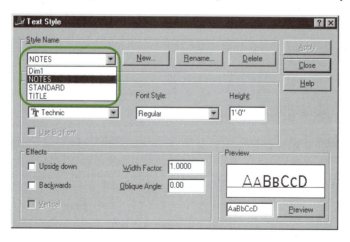

3. Click the style that you wish to make current.

4. Click the Close button.

Using Single-Line Text

For single letters, words, or short sentences and notes, AutoCAD offers single-line text. Each line of text, whether it consists of one letter or several words, behaves as a single item. You can make multiple lines of text with single-line text, but the text won't **word-wrap** at a predefined margin, as it will with AutoCAD's multiline text or in a word-processing program.

Putting Single-Line Text into a Drawing

To use single-line text, you start by specifying a point in the drawing to begin the text, and deciding whether the text will be placed with an orientation other than horizontal.

1. Click Draw ➢ Text ➢ Single Line Text. In the Command window, you will see the name of the current text style and its height, and you will be prompted to pick a point or select one of two options: Style or Justify.

2. Pick a point in the drawing to serve as the lower-left corner of a new line of text. The Command window now gives you the options of accepting the default angle of rotation of the text (0.00) or entering a different angle. Press ↵ to accept the default of no rotation.

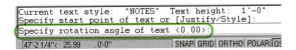

Word-wrap
A feature of most word-processing programs in which words are automatically placed on the next line below when a line exceeds a set length.

The Style option allows you to change the current style. The Justify option is discussed in the next section.

Use the Rotation option when you want your text to follow a sloping line.

179

With single-line text, the new text appears in your drawing as you type it.

3. A text prompt appears in your drawing at the point you picked in the previous step. Type in your new text. The prompt stays to the right of the new text.

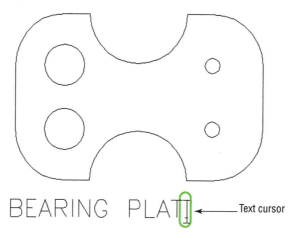

BEARING PLAT◻ ← Text cursor

4. When finished, press ↵. The text cursor jumps one line down and sits at the beginning of a new line of text.

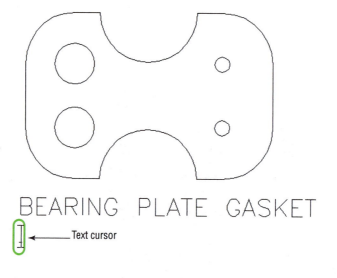

BEARING PLATE GASKET

◻ ← Text cursor

When using single-line text, pressing ↵ twice will end the command.

5. Press ↵ a second time to end the Single Line Text command, or type in a second line of text, and then press ↵ twice.

Using a New Justification Point

Text justification point
A point associated with a line of single-line text that is used to locate that text in the drawing. Each line of text has 12 possible justification points.

If you want your single-line text to be centered inside a circle, for example, use the Justification option to change the **text justification point**.

1. After starting the Single Line Text command, type **j** ↵. The Command window displays all the justification options.

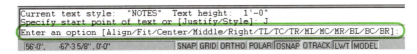

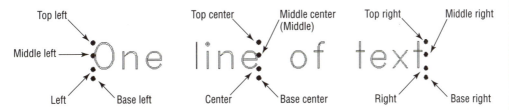

The 12 justification points each define the position of the insertion point relative to the text. TL, for example, places the insertion point at the top-left of the text area.

2. Type **m** ↵ to select the Middle justification. The graphic below shows the 12 possible justification points for single-line text.

3. Choose the Center Osnap from the Object Snap flyout on the Standard toolbar.

4. Click on the circle.

5. Press ↵ for the rotation option.

6. Type in the letter or word to be centered in the circle.

7. Press ↵ twice. The text is centered and the Single Line Text command ends.

The text won't appear centered until you press ↵ for the second time and end the command.

See Also For more information on object snaps, see Chapter 7: "Achieving Precision with the Object Snap Tools."

Changing the Wording of Single-Line Text

When you need to make changes in the wording of single-line text in your drawing, you have a handy tool at your disposal.

1. Click Modify ➢ Text on the pull-down menus.

2. Then click on the line of text you wish to change. The Edit Text dialog box comes up and displays the text you selected. The text is highlighted.

3. Make any changes necessary and click OK. The text is modified in your drawing and you are prompted to select another line of text for editing.

The Modify Text command keeps running until you end it.

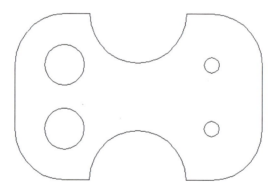

BEARING PLATE TEMPLATE

4. Repeat steps 2 and 3 to modify more text, or press ↵ to end the command.

This method can be used to modify only one line of text at a time.

Changing Any Aspect of Single-Line Text

If you need to change a property of single-line text other than its wording, use the Properties window.

1. Click the line of text that you wish to modify. A grip will appear at its justification point.

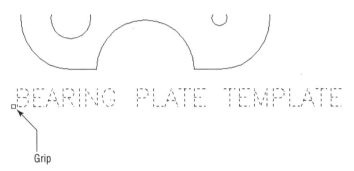

Grip

2. Click the Properties button on the Standard toolbar.

3. In the Properties window, note the list of **text properties** and their current values after the list of General properties.

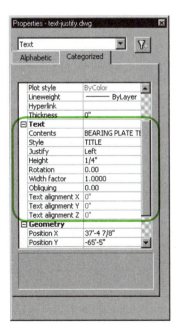

This method for modifying text can be used for more than one line of text at a time.

Text properties
The various characteristics that define the appearance of text, such as height, font, width factor, etc. The text style settings define the properties.

If multiple lines of single-line text have been selected for modification, the Properties window will display only those property values that all the selected lines have in common.

183

4. Click the Text property that you wish to change.

Tip

The Properties window can be used to modify the wording of the text, but if that is all you wish to do, it's easier and quicker to use the Modify Text method described in the previous section.

5. Click again on the current value for that property and make the necessary change.

6. Close the Properties window by clicking its X in the upper-right corner.

7. Press the Esc key twice to remove the grip from the modified text.

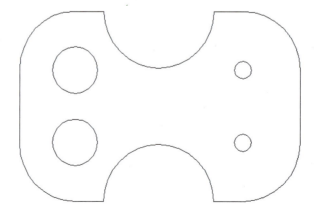

BEARING PLATE TEMPLATE

Using Multiline Text

For notes and paragraphs of text, use multiline text (or mtext, for short). This text is placed in your drawing using the Multiline Text command. The icon for this command is at the bottom of the Draw toolbar.

When you use this command, you are first prompted to pick two points to create a **controlling rectangle**, the sides of which will control how long each line of mtext can be.

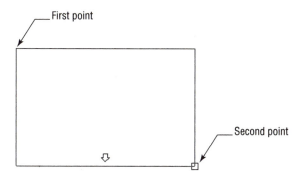

First point

Second point

Then the Multiline Text Editor comes up. It has four tabs of settings, several buttons, and a large blank area where you will enter your text.

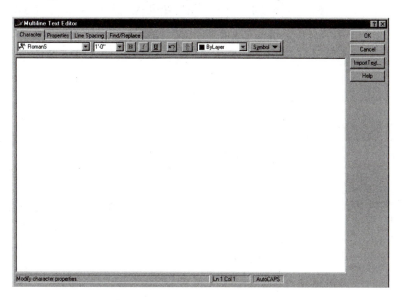

Controlling rectangle

In mtext, a rectangle that encompasses the mtext. It is created by the user at the beginning of the Mtext command, and its width is the line width for the mtext. Its height will change depending on how much text is used.

Click the Help button in the Multiline Text Editor to find out about all the tabs and other buttons.

Use the Multiline Text Editor like a word processor when you enter your text. When you have finished typing, and have pressed the OK button, the text will be placed into your drawing.

Tip

Don't worry about the height of the controlling rectangle limiting the amount of text you can enter. If you type in more text than can fit in the rectangle, the rectangle just drops down (or up, depending on the justification point) to accommodate.

You can easily modify the line length of mtext using grips. When you click on a letter, all the text is selected. It is ghosted, and grips appear at each of the four corners of the body of mtext.

A body of mtext behaves like a single object.

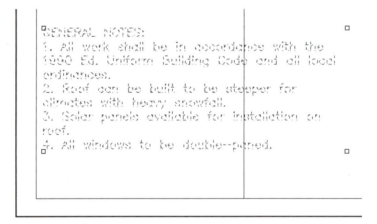

When you click on one of the grips to make it hot, and then stretch it to the left or right, the controlling rectangle appears and changes shape as the crosshair moves.

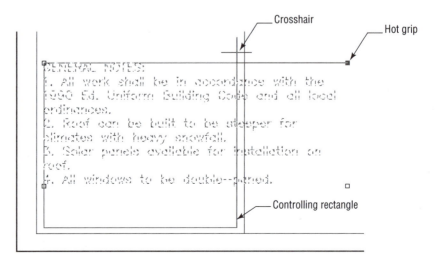

See Also   You can also use the grips to move the paragraph to a new location without changing its line length. See Chapter 8: "Selecting Lines and Other Items in Your Drawing."

This results in a change in the line length for all the text. The body of text is thereby resized.

```
GENERAL NOTES:
1. All work shall be in
accordance with the 1990 Ed.
Uniform Building Code and all
local ordinances.
2. Roof can be built to be
steeper for climates with
heavy snowfall.
3. Solar panels available for
installation on roof.
4. All windows to be
double-paned.
```

Other features of multiline text include the following:

- Individual letters or words can have different properties (height, color, etc.) than the main body of text.

- The Properties window and the Modify Text command, discussed in previous sections of this chapter, can both be used to modify mtext. When modifying mtext, you use the same Multiline Text Editor that you used to first type in the text.

- Special characters like the symbols for diameter and degrees can be inserted into mtext.

- Mtext can be converted into single-line text.

- Whole documents made with a word-processing program can be imported into AutoCAD as mtext.

Summary

This chapter demonstrated the basic procedures for setting up a new text style and working with single-line text and gave a brief description of AutoCAD's Multiline Text feature. For more in-depth instruction in the methods of controlling text in your drawing, see either of two Sybex books: *Mastering AutoCAD 2000*, by George Omura, or *AutoCAD 2000, No Experience Required* by this author.

Chapter 13

Dimensions

Most technical drawings need to show dimensions for at least a few elements; so even though the dimensioning tools of AutoCAD are complex and usually treated as an intermediate-level feature of the program, it seems appropriate to include an introduction to the subject in this book. This chapter will first touch on the basic types of dimensions and the tools available for inserting them and then briefly look at the general techniques for styling dimensions as you want them to appear in your drawing.

- ◆ Using linear dimensions
- ◆ Placing angular dimensions
- ◆ Creating radial dimensions
- ◆ Making leaders
- ◆ Creating a new dimension style
- ◆ Modifying an existing dimension style

Putting Dimensions on a Drawing

This section introduces the tools that AutoCAD provides for working with the three basic types of dimensions:

- Linear, for measuring distances between two points

- Angular, for measuring angles and arcs

- Radial, for measuring radii and diameters

Each type uses some of AutoCAD's dimensioning tools, and some of those tools can be used on more than one dimension type. All dimensions have in common the feature that, as a dimension is placed in the drawing, AutoCAD calculates the distance or angle and uses that measurement for the dimension text. You can change the text manually if you want, but initially the text shows the results of the measurement. As a result, the process of dimensioning is also a process of checking the accuracy of your drawing.

Linear and angular dimensions consist of four parts that are illustrated in the diagram below. We'll look at each of these parts in the discussion that follows.

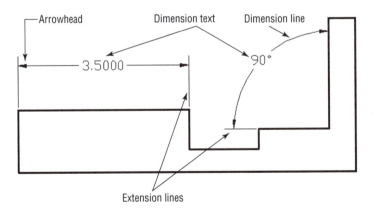

The illustrations in this chapter use the default settings that control a dimension's appearance, so they may look different from the ones you are used to using. Later in this chapter, you'll learn how to adjust the default settings and thereby create your own custom dimension style.

We'll begin by bringing the Dimension toolbar onto the screen.

Displaying the Dimension Toolbar

You will find it handy to have the Dimension toolbar on your screen while placing dimensions on the drawing.

1. Right-click any button on a toolbar to bring up the Toolbar menu.

2. Click the Dimension option.

3. Drag the toolbar to the top of the drawing area.

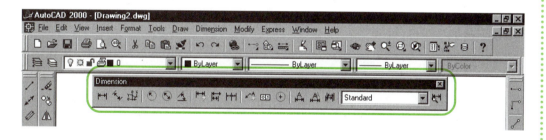

See Also You can dock the Dimension toolbar outside the drawing area just like any toolbar, but you may not need it on the screen except when you are putting dimensions on a drawing. See Chapter 1 for information on docking toolbars.

Each trade or profession that uses dimensions in drawings has its own style of presenting them. The many settings that control the dimension's appearance provide the means for AutoCAD to satisfy almost all of these drafting styles.

Horizontal and Vertical Dimensions

There are several tools to help you dimension linear distances. The first one that we'll look at, Linear, is used for a single horizontal or vertical dimension. To use it, you pick two points or select a line that extends between the two points you wish to dimension. AutoCAD calculates the distance between them and displays it in the default or current dimension style.

1. Click the Linear button on the Dimension toolbar.

The two points picked in the illustration are separated by both a horizontal and a vertical distance, in order to demonstrate dimensions in both directions. If the two points instead have a simple horizontal or vertical line between them, you can pick that line instead of the line's two endpoints. To do this, right-click after starting the command, and then select the line.

2. In a drawing similar to the one illustrated below, pick the first point, using an Osnap if possible. Then pick the second point.

3. Move the cursor up from the shape. The new horizontal dimension moves with the crosshair cursor.

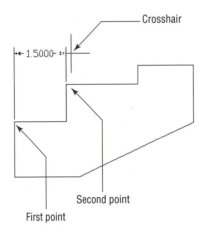

After the dimension appears, and before its location is fixed, you can change the dimension text (Type **m** ↵) or its angle relative to the dimension line (type **a** ↵).

4. Move the cursor out to the left of the shape. A vertical dimension replaces the horizontal one, and it follows the crosshair.

Note

You are able to get the results in step 4 because the two points you picked were not lined up horizontally or vertically. If they were lined up along either axis, you could display only a horizontal or vertical linear dimension.

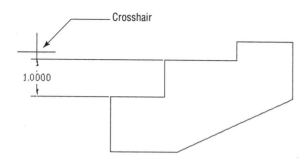

5. Move the crosshair back to a position above the shape and, when the dimension is in a good location, click to fix it there and end the Linear Dimension command.

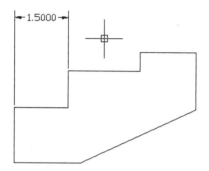

Continued Dimensions

Once a single dimension has been placed in a drawing, if there is a need for more dimensions to be placed in such a way that the **dimension lines** of the new dimension line up with those of the first, use the Continue option.

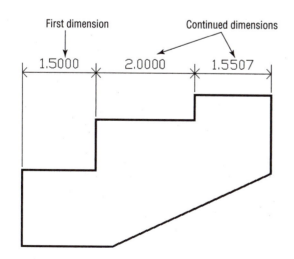

Dimension line
The line that extends between the arrowheads and shows the direction in which the dimension has been measured.

The Continue option can be used for both linear and angular dimensions.

1. Click the Continue Dimension button on the Dimension toolbar.

2. The cursor now has a new dimension attached to it; the value changes as the cursor is moved. Click the next point above and to the right of the last point. A second dimension is drawn, and a third one appears that is attached to the cursor again.

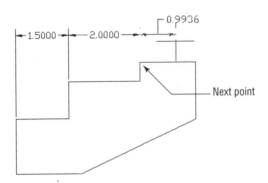

Extension line

The line that extends from the dimensioned object to the dimension line. They are usually perpendicular to the dimension line.

Tip

When you use the Continue option, AutoCAD assumes that the new dimensions are to be lined up with the last dimension that was placed. If you wish to use Continue on a different dimension, right-click after starting the option and click the **extension line** that you want the Continue option to work from.

The Continue option keeps running until you stop it by pressing the Esc key or right-clicking a couple of times.

3. Click the upper-right corner of the shape to place the third dimension. To end Continue, press the Esc key or right-click twice.

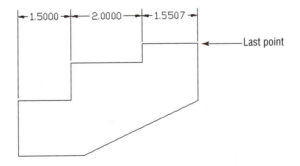

Baseline Dimensions

Another dimensioning option that is similar to Continue is the Baseline option. It works the same way as continued dimensioning, but it places each new dimension above the last dimension and measures all dimensions from the same **base point**.

1. Once you have placed the first linear dimension, click the Baseline Dimension button on the Dimension toolbar.

2. A baseline dimension appears above the first dimension; it is attached to the cursor.

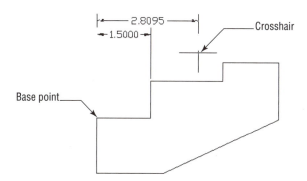

3. Pick the second point of the dimension.

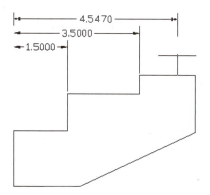

4. Pick the upper-right corner of the shape to place the second baseline dimension, and then right-click twice to end the Baseline option.

Base point

In dimensioning, the point from which a group of baseline dimensions are all started.

With baseline dimensions, AutoCAD automatically selects the first point of the last dimension you made as the base point. If you want a different base point, right-click after step 1 to activate the Select option, and then select the extension line that is attached to the point you want for the base point.

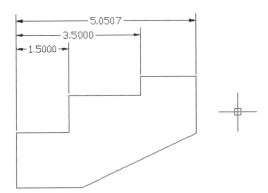

Tip

The Baseline dimension tool is often used to place an overall dimension above a series of continued dimensions. To use it in this way, use the Select option after the Baseline command has begun and select the extension line at one end of the set of continued dimensions.

Quick Dimensions

The Quick Dimension feature automatically creates several horizontal or vertical dimensions at once. It lines the dimension lines up like the Continue option discussed above. This tool can save you lots of time.

1. Click the Quick Dimension button on the Dimension toolbar.

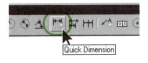

2. Select the objects in the drawing that you wish to dimension and press ↵.

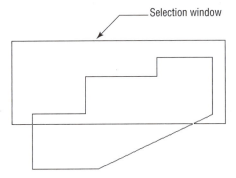

3. The command window now displays various options, with Continuous being the default. You can remove any of the selected vertices that you don't want dimensioned. Type **e** ↵ to select the Edit option. All vertices within the selection are displayed with a cross.

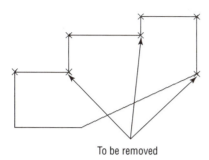

To be removed

4. Click each selected vertex that should not be dimensioned, to remove it from the selection. Then right-click. Move the crosshair cursor to the place where you want the dimension lines to be placed.

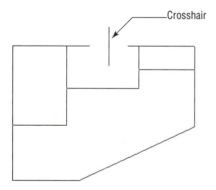

Crosshair

The Edit option has an Add option that allows you to add vertices to the original selection.

5. Click to fix the dimension line location and complete the Quick Dimension command.

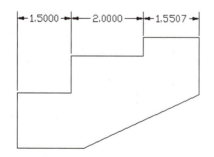

1.5000   2.0000   1.5507

Whether you decide to use Quick Dimension or not will depend on the complexity of the part of your drawing you are dimensioning. The more complicated the geometry, the more time you will have to spend deleting vertices, and the less useful Quick Dimension becomes.

Aligned Dimensions

When you need to dimension a line or a distance that is not horizontal or vertical, use the Aligned option. You can pick two points or, if you are dimensioning a line, select the line itself and let AutoCAD find its endpoints. AutoCAD will position the extension lines perpendicular to the line (or to an imaginary line between the two points). Follow these steps to select the line itself.

1. Click the Aligned Dimension button on the Dimension toolbar.

2. At the `Specify first extension line origin or <select object>:` prompt, right-click to use the Select Object option.

3. Select the line to be dimensioned. The dimension is displayed in ghosted fashion and moves away from the line as the cursor is moved.

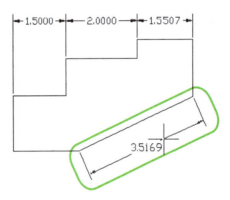

4. Use the cursor to position the dimension where you want it; then click to both fix it there and end the command.

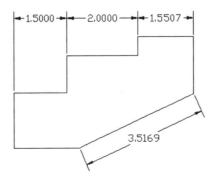

For linear dimensions, Auto-CAD always makes the extension lines perpendicular to the dimension line. The Oblique command on the Dimension pull-down menu allows the angle between the extension lines and dimension line to be greater or less than 90. However, it's only used in specialized situations.

Angular Dimensions

The Angular Dimension tool allows you to dimension the angle between any two nonparallel lines, two points on a circle, an arc, or between any three points. The steps that follow illustrate the first of these options, but they all work in a similar fashion. The differences between the options will be listed afterwards.

1. Click the Angular Dimension button on the Dimension toolbar.

2. Select a line.

3. Select another line that forms an angle with the first one.

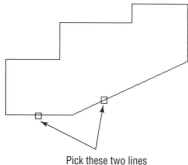

Pick these two lines

4. Move the cursor around and notice how the angular dimension slides along the two lines.

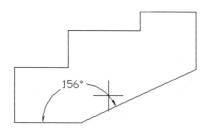

If you move the cursor and dimension across one of the lines that form the angle, the dimension will change to reflect the complement of the original angle. (In our example, it would show the "outside" angle, 24°.) Try it.

5. When you have positioned the dimension where you want it, click to fix it there and end the command.

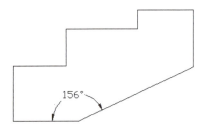

If you are dimensioning an angle of a circle, an arc, or an angle formed by three points, use the above procedure with the following variations:

◆ For a circle, after the command has begun, click two points on the circle, and then place the dimension inside or outside the circle.

◆ For an arc, after the command has begun, select the arc, and then place the dimension inside or outside the arc.

◆ For three points, start the command, and then right-click to use the Vertex option. You will then be prompted to pick one of the points to be the **vertex** and then the other two. To finish, place the dimension as in the procedure above.

Vertex
The point where two line segments meet. For angles, the vertex is the place where the two lines that form the angle meet, or would meet.

Radial Dimensions

AutoCAD offers tools for creating Radius and Diameter dimensions. They work about the same way, so we will look at the Radius tool and you can try the Diameter tool on your own. One of the most common uses of the radius dimension is to show the radius of a filleted corner.

1. Click the Radius Dimension button on the Dimension toolbar.

The Diameter Dimension button is just to the right of the Radius Dimension button, and the two icons are similar.

2. Click on the arc that forms the fillet. A radius dimension appears, and its text is attached to the cursor.

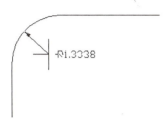

3. Move the cursor inside or outside the arc to see the various ways the dimension looks.

4. When you have the dimension where you want it, click to fix it in that location and end the command.

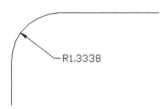

If you locate the dimension text outside the filleted corner, a cross is automatically placed at the center point of the arc that makes up the fillet.

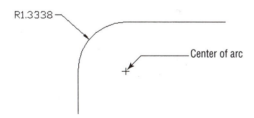

If you place a radial dimension inside an arc or circle but also want a cross at its center, click the Center Mark button on the Dimension toolbar and, using the Center Object snap, click the arc or circle.

Leader

An arrow or dot with a line that connects text information about an object to that object.

A leader line can be a series of straight-line segments or a curved line made up of a spline curve.

Making Leaders

Chapter 12 showed how to add notes or annotations to AutoCAD drawings. Many notes require **leaders** that reference a point or shape in the drawing. The Quick Leader tool allows you to add these notes with leaders. There are more options for making leaders than there is room to present in this book, but you can get started using them without having to know all about all the options. I will demonstrate a simple leader using default settings, and then mention some of the options that you may want to investigate on your own.

1. Click the Quick Leader button on the Dimension toolbar.

2. You can pick a point to locate the tip of the arrowhead, or press ↵ to see a dialog box of leader settings. To accept the default settings, pick a point to locate the arrowhead. Use an Osnap if you need to.

3. Move the cursor to a place where you would like the first leader segment to end.

4. Click to set the second point. Now you can stop adding segments or continue picking points to make more. We will stop here, so press ↵ to stop making segments.

5. Next you are prompted to pick a point or enter a number to set the maximum length of a line of note text. Pick that point or type in a distance.

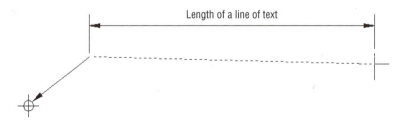

Length of a line of text

See Also Leaders use Multiline text. The basic techniques for using this kind of text are introduced in Chapter 12, "Putting Text into a Drawing."

6. Type in the text, and then press ↵. You can type in a second line if necessary or finish by pressing ↵ again. For this exercise, press ↵. The command ends and the text is placed next to the leader line.

Once the leader is on the drawing, you can use grips to adjust the position and length of the text, as well as the length and direction of the leader line.

If you press ↵ after beginning the Quick Leader command, the Leader Settings dialog box comes up.

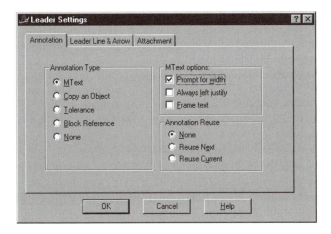

It has three tabs that do the following:

◆ Annotation, for controlling the type of **annotation** used in the leader

◆ Leader Line & Arrow, for specifying the type of line used for a leader, the type of arrowhead, the number of line segments allowable, and the angles allowable for the lines

◆ Attachment, for choosing where the end of the leader meets the text

If the last leader line segment makes an angle greater than 15° above or below the horizontal, AutoCAD automatically adds a short horizontal line segment, called a "dog leg," between the end of the leader line and the text.

Annotation
Notes or other forms of readable information used in a drawing.

Setting Up a Dimension Style

The preceding section introduced the basic types of dimensions, using the default settings that control the dimension's appearance. These settings are grouped into a dimension style called the Standard style, which comes with every new AutoCAD drawing. To make modifications to the way dimensions appear, you create a new style from the Standard style and then make changes to its settings.

This section shows the procedure for creating a new dimension style and changing its settings. Then I will list some of the things about a dimension's appearance you may want to make and note where you can make them.

Creating a New Dimension Style

To create a new dimension style, you first make a copy of the Standard style and rename it.

1. Click the Dimension Style button at the right end of the Dimension toolbar.

A drawing can contain any number of dimension styles.

2. The Dimension Style Manager dialog box comes up. Note the following features:

   ◇ The upper-left corner shows the Current Dimstyle (dimension style).

   ◇ Below that is a large list box showing the dimension styles saved with the current drawing.

   ◇ To the right, a preview window shows how the various types of dimensions will appear under the settings of the current style.

The preview window will become useful later in the chapter, when you begin modifying the new dimension style.

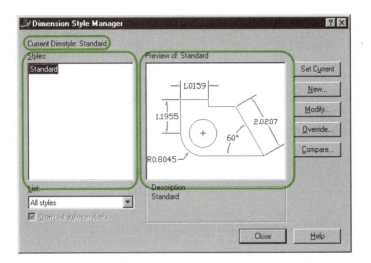

3. Click the New button on the right side of the dialog box. This will bring up the Create New Dimension Style dialog box.

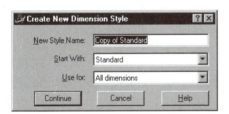

4. In the New Style Name text box, Copy of Standard is highlighted. Type in **DIM1**, the arbitrary name we'll use for our new dimension style.

5. The Start With drop-down list displays Standard. This means the new style will be a copy of Standard. This is what we want. Click Continue.

6. Next a large dialog box comes up. It has six tabs and is titled "New Dimension Style: DIM1." We will work with this dialog box in the next section. For now, click OK.

A new dimension style is always created as a copy of an existing, or predefined, dimension style, usually the Standard style. For this reason, it is important to always preserve the original Standard dimension style. New dimension styles are based on the Standard style, so leaving the Standard style alone is important.

The first time the dialog box comes up for a new style, it is called New Dimension Style. After that, its name changes to Modify Dimension Style. Both also carry the name of the new style (DIM1) or the name of the style being modified.

The preview of the DIM1 style is identical to that of the Standard style because, at this point, the setting values for both are identical.

7. Back in the Dimension Style Manager dialog box, DIM1 now appears in the list of Dimension Styles, and it is previewed in the Preview Of: window. Click the Close button to return to your drawing.

Making Modifications to a Dimension Style

In the preceding section, you created a new dimension style by making a copy of the default Standard style, and named it DIM1 or another name of your choosing. Now you will see how to modify settings in the new style to make a custom style that fits your purposes.

1. Click the Dimension Style button on the Dimension toolbar.

2. In the Styles list, Standard is highlighted because it is still the current style. Highlight DIM1 in the Styles list and click the Modify button on the right side. The Modify Dimension Style: DIM1 dialog box comes up.

3. Lines and Arrows should be the active tab. If it's not, click it. Note the preview window that matches the one in the Dimension Style Manager dialog box.

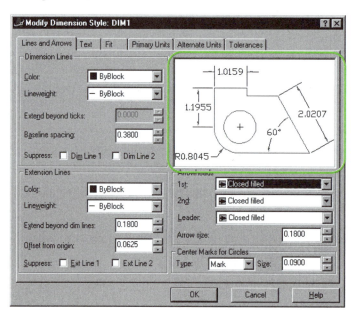

Tip

The Preview window is repeated on each of the six tabs of the Modify Dimension Style dialog box. It is a useful visual tool for learning about the dimension settings because you can see the results of each change you make in the settings.

4. In the Arrowheads section below the Preview window, click the 1st list box to open it.

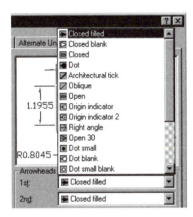

5. Click the Right Angle choice and notice what happens after the list closes:

◇ Both the 1st and 2nd arrowhead list boxes display Right Angle.

◇ In the preview window, the arrowheads have changed from Closed Filled to Right Angle arrowheads.

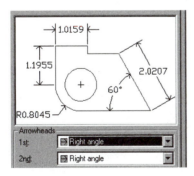

That's the only change we'll make on this tab.

6. Click the Text tab. We'll be making changes in the Text Placement and Text Alignment areas, while keeping an eye on the preview window.

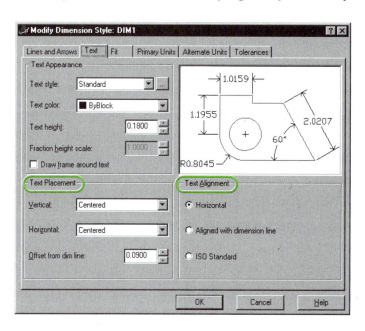

The default Horizontal choice for Text Alignment forces all dimension text to be horizontal, regardless of the orientation of the dimension line.

7. In the Text Alignment area, select Aligned with Dimension Line. Note how the dimension text now lines up with the dimension lines.

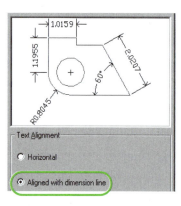

208

8. In the Text Placement area, open the Vertical drop-down list and select Above. Note how the text in the preview window is now above each dimension line.

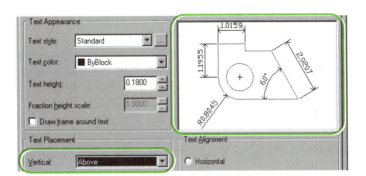

In the Text Placement area, the default Vertical setting is Centered. This choice will place the text right on the dimension line and break the line around the text.

9. These are the only changes we will make for this new style. Click OK to close the Modify Dimension Style dialog box.

10. Back in the Dimension Style Manager dialog box, make sure DIM1 is highlighted in the Styles list. The Preview window will display the dimensions as they appear in the highlighted dimension style, DIM1. Click the Set Current button to make DIM 1 the **current dimension style**.

Current dimension style

The dimension style that controls how new dimensions appear in a drawing.

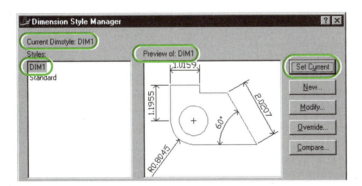

11. Click the Close button at the bottom of the Dimension Style Manager dialog box and return to your drawing.

In the last section of the chapter, you will learn how to update a dimension in your drawing to match the current style.

Other Dimension Settings You May Want to Change

There are over fifty settings that control the appearances of dimensions. You have been introduced to the basic procedure for changing settings, and you've seen how to change three of them. Here are some further settings that a beginner may want to change to make a custom dimension style. They are grouped by the tabs that contain the settings.

Lines and Arrows

On the Lines and Arrows tab, you may want to try any of the following:

- Using a different arrowhead.

- Adjusting Baseline Offset dimension—this is the Baseline Spacing setting. It controls how far above the previous dimension the baseline dimension is positioned.

- Leader line arrow—you can assign an arrowhead for leaders that is different than the one assigned to the other kinds of dimensions.

Text

On the Text tab, you may want to try either of the following:

- New Text Style for dimension text—you can choose any previously defined text style to be the one used for dimensions.

- Adjust text height—this controls the height of the dimension text. It overrides the height set for the text style.

Fit

There is only one adjustment you should consider on the Fit tab:

- Set overall scale—most drawings require you to set a scale factor here that reflects the scale factor at which your drawing will be printed.

See Also Printing scale factors are discussed further in Chapter 15, "Printing a Drawing."

Primary Units

On the Primary Units tab, you can make these adjustments:

⬥ Set the Linear and Angular Units

⬥ Set the Linear and Angular Precision

⬥ Zero Suppression: in Architectural units, the default style is to show both feet and inches, even if one of them has a zero value. You can have AutoCAD not show 0' or 0" (for example, 12' instead of 12'-0", or 7" instead of 0'-7"). In decimal units, the default style for numbers less than 1 is to display a 0 before the decimal point, but you can choose to display them without the 0 (for example, .75 instead of 0.75). If one or more decimal places are required in the precision setting, integers can be displayed without the decimal point and the zeros to the right (for example, 75 instead of 75.0).

Updating Dimensions to Conform to the Current Dimension Style

Dimensions in a drawing may have been made using a dimension style other than the style that is now current, or using the current style before it was modified. You can use the Update command to bring these dimensions into conformity with the modified settings of the current dimension style. In the first part of the chapter, we used a diagram to illustrate linear and angular dimensions. For those dimensions, we used the default Standard dimension style. Now we will update those dimensions to conform to the new settings for the DIM1 style.

1. Start with the diagram that showed linear and angular dimensions, including baseline and continued dimensions.

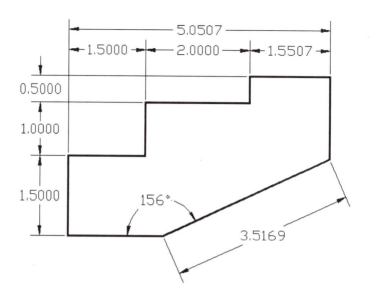

2. On the Dimension toolbar, be sure the DIM1 style is displayed on the Dimension Style Control list, indicating that it is the current dimension style. If it's not, open the list and click on DIM1 to make it current.

3. Click Dimension ➢ Update on the pull-down menus.

4. Select all dimensions needing to be updated, then press ↵.

5. The dimensions will be automatically updated to conform to the "latest edition" of the current dimension style.

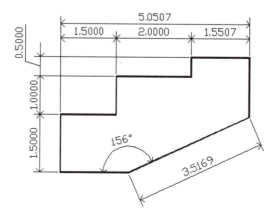

Summary

This chapter has been an introduction to the dimensioning features of AutoCAD. We have looked at the tools used to create the basic dimension types and the techniques for creating new, custom dimension styles. You've also seen how to update dimensions to conform to the current dimension style. Individual dimensions can also be modified in various ways: using grips, dimension style overrides, and any of a number of commands and features, but this subject is beyond the scope of this book. To learn more about dimensions, look at Sybex's other books on AutoCAD. *AutoCAD 2000: No Experience Required*, by this author, extends this introduction by covering some intermediate features of dimensioning. *Mastering AutoCAD 2000*, by George Omura, is a comprehensive reference that covers dimensioning in depth.

Chapter 14

Using Blocks in a Drawing

A block is any grouping of objects that you work with as a single unit in order to use it repeatedly, either in one drawing or in multiple drawings. Nearly all AutoCAD drawings use blocks. Some of these are drawing symbols like a north arrow or a section cut line. Others are specific to a trade, such as furniture symbols in interior design, trees in landscape architecture, or a switch in an electrical layout. You can buy predefined collections of blocks (known as symbol libraries) for various fields, or you can create your own blocks. To create a block, you first draw the objects and then group them into a block. Once you've done that, you can easily reproduce the block several times, move it around in the drawing, and use it in other drawings.

- Drawing a symbol to use for a block
- Creating a block
- Inserting a block
- Using AutoCAD Design Center to get a block from another drawing
- Making a drawing file out of a block

What Should Be a Block?

In general, any group of lines or other objects that will be used over and over again in your drawings is a good candidate to be made into a **block**. Here are some common examples.

Office chair Plant Drawing symbol Electrical symbol

Creating a Block

To create a block, you first draw the objects that you wish to include in it. Then use the Block command to convert these items into a block. Each block has a reference point called the **insertion point** that you use to locate the block in the drawing.

Drawing a Symbol

When you draw the lines that will make up the new block, use the Draw commands that were introduced in Chapter 3. Here's a summary of the process, using a drawing of a north arrow **symbol**. You can draw it if you like, or draw your own symbol.

1. Be sure the 0 layer is current. To do this, check the Layer Control dropdown list to see if the 0 layer is displayed. If it is not, open the list and click the 0 layer.

2. If there are any lines already existing in the drawing that you want to be part of your block, use the Property Manager to move these items onto the 0 layer.

3. Draw any new lines that will be in the block. For the north arrow, start with a circle that has a radius of 2 units. Then follow the five steps below.

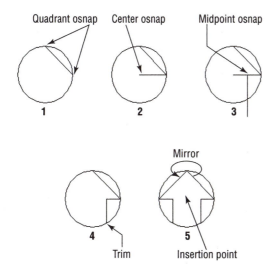

4. Determine where the insertion point should be, and draw any guide-lines necessary to locate this point. (No guidelines are necessary for the north arrow, because the insertion point will be the center of the circle.)

Now you are ready to make the block. Go on to the next section.

Creating a Block from a Symbol

Creating a new block requires that you name the block, specify an insertion point, and select the items to include in the block. Then you have a couple of further options. The following is a summary of the process.

1. Click the Make Block button on the Draw toolbar.

2. In the Block Definition dialog box, do the following:

   ◇ Enter a name for the block.

   ◇ In the Base Point area, click the Pick Point button and, in your drawing, pick a point to be the insertion point. (Use object snaps if necessary.)

   ◇ In the Objects area, first click the Select Objects button and, in your drawing, select those objects to be part of the block. Then press ↵.

   ◇ Back in the Objects area of the Block Definition dialog box, choose a radio button to: Retain the objects you selected after the block is made, Convert the lines into the new block, or Delete the lines.

   ◇ In the Preview Icon area, click the lower radio button to save a picture of the block.

   ◇ Click OK. The block is made and stored in your drawing file.

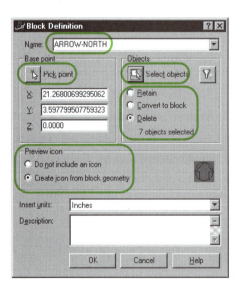

Working with Blocks in the Drawing

Once a block has been created, it is stored invisibly in your drawing as a **block definition**, and saved there. Then a **block reference** that is based upon that

---

Blocks can be named for the thing they represent, like "CHAIR," be code-named, as in "CH-OFF-1," or use a combination of the two, as in "CHAIR-OFF-1." If you have many chair blocks, you will need a code-naming system.

Use the Retain option to generate more blocks that are variations of the first one, or if you need to use the objects independently. Use Convert to Block if the selected objects are already positioned where the blocks should be. You will then have to move the new block to the proper layer. Use Delete if the new block will be positioned elsewhere.

The Insert Units option in the lower half of the Block Definition dialog box is an optional setting that allows you to specify the units to which a block is scaled when it is inserted. If a block was created in architectural units and is inserted into a drawing that uses metric units, for example, this setting is important. If left alone, the default units are the units of the current drawing. We'll leave it alone.

definition can be inserted into the drawing. Blocks can also be transferred to other drawings or to a library folder.

Inserting a Block into a Drawing

To place a block in your drawing, use the Insert command to select the block and set the parameters for the block's location, size and orientation in the drawing. The following exercise shows how the insertion process works. If you created a block in the previous section, you can insert it now. If not, you can apply the process to any block you have created or otherwise obtained.

1. Make sure the layer where you wish to insert the block is current.

2. Click the Insert button on the Draw toolbar.

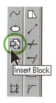

3. Use the Insert dialog box to:

   ◇ Select a block from the Name drop-down list.

   ◇ Specify the insertion point location, scale, and rotation or choose to set these On-Screen.

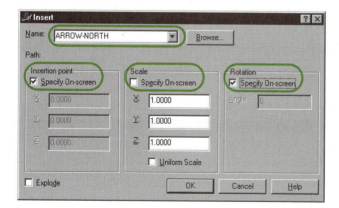

4. Click OK. If you chose to set any of the **insertion parameters** on-screen, you will be prompted for those settings in the command window.

Block definition

The information about a block that is saved with the drawing and used to insert the block into the drawing. This information is the block's name, its insertion point location, and the geometric description of the objects that make up the block. This information is saved in the drawing even though you may not see the actual block on the screen.

Block reference

A representation of a block definition that is visible in the drawing. It is placed in the drawing with the Insert command.

If the blocks you are inserting all have the same insertion point location and you know its coordinates—0,0 for example—or all have the same scale or rotation, presetting these in the Insert dialog box will save you time. Otherwise, you will have to specify these or accept the defaults for them on-screen.

Insertion parameters

The three settings for defining the location (Insertion Point), size (Scale), and orientation (Rotation) of a block reference.

219

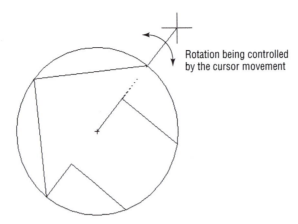

Rotation being controlled
by the cursor movement

5. When all the parameters are set, the block is inserted.

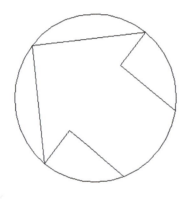

The rotation of a block can be set on-screen by rotating the crosshair about the insertion point or by entering an angle. If Ortho is on, the block can only be rotated by the cursor in 90-degree increments.

Retrieving a Block from Another Drawing

Often you will want to pull a block out of another drawing and use it in your current drawing. The AutoCAD DesignCenter feature makes this easy; the drawing that contains the block doesn't even have to be open. If you have the Sample folder that comes with AutoCAD 2000, you should be able to do this exercise. Otherwise, any AutoCAD drawing with blocks will do.

The AutoCAD DesignCenter window stays on your screen until you click its Close (X) button. It can be docked on either side of the drawing area and resized, and it has several additional features that are beyond the scope of this book.

1. Click File ➢ New to open a new drawing. Then click the AutoCAD DesignCenter button on the Standard toolbar.

2. In the DesignCenter window, use the left side to find the Acad2000 folder and open the Sample sub-folder to view the drawings in that folder.

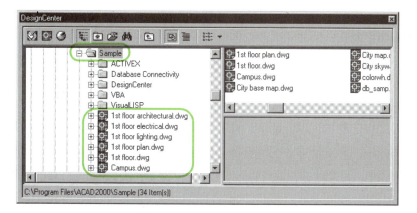

3. Click the + symbol to the left of the 1st floor plan.dwg file. A list of types of items that may be copied appears below the drawing name.

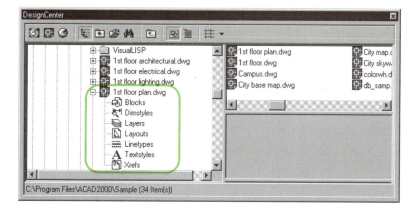

4. In the list, highlight Blocks. A list of the blocks in the drawing appears on the right side of the DesignCenter window.

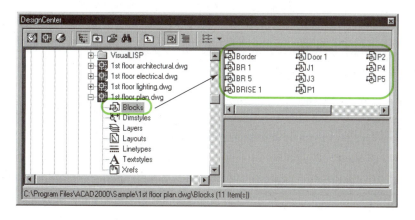

AutoCAD DesignCenter is a powerful feature that enables you to pull blocks, layers, text styles, linetypes, and other elements from unopened drawings and drop them into your current drawing.

5. Highlight the P1 block and view a preview icon of that block in the window below the list of blocks. Enlarge the window to get a better view, if necessary.

To adjust the size of the preview window, hold the cursor on the edge of the window. When the double-arrow resize icon appears, hold down the left mouse button and move the edge of the window. Then release the button.

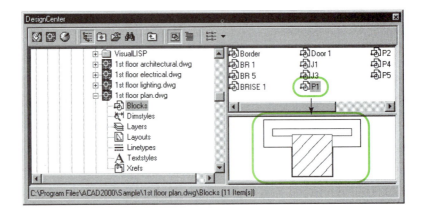

6. When you have the block you want, double-click on the block's name. The Insert dialog box comes up with P1 in the name box.

You can also just drag the block from the Design Center into your drawing. When you do it this way, the Insert dialog box does not come up and the block is copied as-is into your drawing.

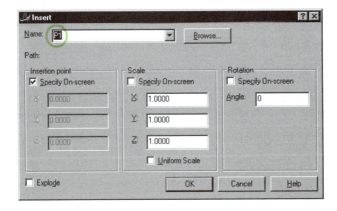

7. Work your way through the insertion process, as discussed in the previous section, and then click OK.

8. Close the DesignCenter window.

9. Complete the block insertion in the new drawing.

When you bring a block into the active drawing from another drawing, the block will bring any layers, linetypes, dimension styles, or text styles that it uses. If the drawing you're inserting into already has any of those elements, they will be used instead.

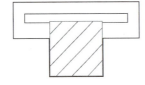

Converting a Block into a Drawing File

Before AutoCAD DesignCenter became part of AutoCAD, the standard method for creating a block library was to make a drawing file out of each block and store them all in a special folder. Sometimes subfolders were used to further classify the blocks. DesignCenter offers an alternative to this method and it is described above, but the process of converting a block into a drawing file is still useful and worth describing. It makes use of the Wblock command, which stands for "write block."

1. Make current the drawing from which you wish to copy the blocks that you'll turn into files.

2. Type **w** ↵. The Write Block dialog box comes up. It is similar to the Insert dialog box discussed above, but there are differences.

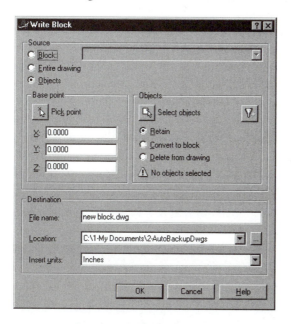

If you click Entire Drawing, a copy of the current drawing will be made into a new drawing file. If you click Objects, you will use the Base Point and Objects tools in the dialog box, and return to your drawing to select a base point and objects to be part of a new drawing file.

3. In the upper-left corner are three radio buttons. These are your choices for the source of the new drawing file. We want to copy a block out of the current drawing, so click Block.

4. Open the drop-down list at the top and select the block you wish to copy and convert to a drawing file. When the list closes, the block's name will appear there and in the File Name text box in the Destination area at the bottom.

5. Use the Location drop-down list or the Browse button to its right to find and select the folder in which you wish to store the new drawing file.

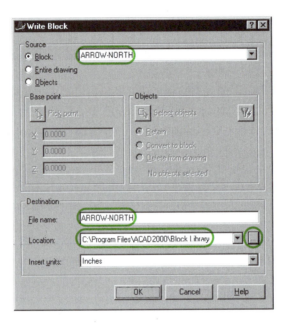

6. Click OK. AutoCAD creates the new file.

7. Click File ➢ Open and navigate to the folder where you stored the new drawing file. It will be listed with the .DWG extension because it is now a drawing.

The Wblock command is also a powerful tool for selecting whole sections in a drawing and creating a new drawing from those selected objects. To do this, choose Objects at the top of the dialog box, instead of Block. The objects that come out bring with them all blocks, layers, linetypes, text styles, and dimension styles that were used for the objects you selected, and these blocks, layers, etc., become part of the new drawing.

Summary

This chapter has been a brief introduction to blocks. It has demonstrated how to create and save blocks from drawn symbols, and how they are inserted into a drawing. I have also included a quick exercise showing how to use AutoCAD DesignCenter to share blocks between drawings, and demonstrated how the Wblock command can be used to create a drawing file from a block. As you begin to develop more complex drawings, you will need to learn more about creating and managing blocks. For further discussion of this topic, see *AutoCAD 2000: No Experience Required*, by this author, and *Mastering AutoCAD 2000*, by George Omura, (1999) Sybex.

Chapter 15

Printing a Drawing

There is usually a feeling of adventure when a beginning AutoCAD user makes a print of their first CAD drawing. While it looks one way on the monitor screen, it will look different on the hard copy, so there is usually an element of surprise. In this chapter, we will look at the basic procedure for printing a drawing, beginning with a discussion on drawing scale.

Printing/plotting has traditionally been one of the trickier aspects of AutoCAD. While ACAD 2000 has streamlined the process, you should still allow for some trial-and-error as you familiarize yourself with the concepts and procedures.

- Determining the best scale for a print
- Selecting a printer
- Setting up a drawing for printing
- Previewing a print

Calculating a Scale for a Drawing

Hard Copy

The printed sheet of paper, as opposed to the electronic file that is displayed on the monitor.

Scale Factor

A number that is associated with a scale and describes the magnitude of change of size from the scaled size to actual size. An object in $\frac{1}{4}$" = 1'-0" scale would be 48 times larger at actual size. So 48 is the scale factor for the $\frac{1}{4}$" = 1'-0" scale.

When you work in AutoCAD, you draw objects at their full size. This means that when you need a line to be 25 feet long, you tell AutoCAD to make the line 25 feet long. When you print a **hard copy** of that line, it has to be scaled down to fit on the paper (unless, of course, your paper is 25 feet long!). We'll look at a method for determining how much a drawing needs to be *scaled down* to fit on the paper that you are using.

There are standard scales used by the various trades and professions that use AutoCAD. Each scale has a ratio called the **scale factor,** which is helpful in sizing a drawing to the paper. Below is a table of standard scales with their scale factors.

Scale	Scale Factor
1" = 1" (Full size)	1
3" = 1'-0"	4
1 unit = 10 units	10
1" = 1'-0"	12
$\frac{1}{4}$" = 1'-0"	48
$\frac{1}{8}$" = 1'-0"	96
1 unit = 100 units	100
1/16" = 1'-0"	192
1" = 40'	480
1" = 100'	1200

Sheet

A trade term for a sheet of paper. Paper used for plotting is often called a sheet.

The scale used for printing is determined by comparing the actual dimensions of the drawing to the **sheet** size.

Determining a Scale for a Sample Drawing

We'll use one of the sample drawings that come with the AutoCAD program and calculate the best scale for printing it on a 36" × 48" sheet. If you have the sample drawing, you can follow the steps. If not, you will still learn about scale by reading along.

1. Click the Open button on the Standard toolbar, navigate to the Sample folder in the Acad2000 directory, and open db_samp.dwg.

2. Make the 0 layer the current layer.

3. Zoom to Extents; then Zoom to .9x.

4. Use the Rectangle command to draw a 36" × 48" rectangle near the lower-left corner of the drawing. This will represent the sheet.

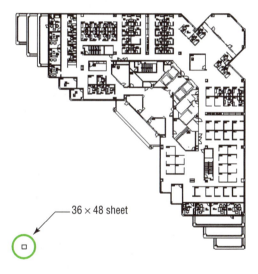

36 × 48 sheet

5. Click the rectangle to select it; then click the grip in the lower-left corner to activate it.

6. Press the spacebar three times to bring up the Scale option.

7. Type **c** ↵ to select the Copy option. Now we'll enter a scale factor from the chart above.

The Copy option is available for each of the five commands that work with grips. When using this option, the command modifies the objects with grips, while preserving the original shape.

By entering a scale factor, you enlarge the rectangle that represents the sheet. The new rectangle can encompass more of the drawing.

8. Type **12** ↵. This will create a rectangle that would represent the area that a 36 × 48 sheet could cover at a scale of 1" = 1'-0". As you can see, it's too small.

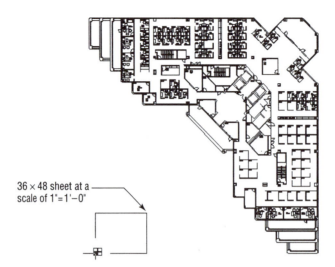

36 × 48 sheet at a scale of 1"=1'−0"

9. Type **48** ↵. This rectangle shows what the same sheet would cover at a scale of 1/4" = 1'-0". It's still too small to contain the entire drawing.

10. Type **96** ↵. This rectangle goes off the screen. It's certainly big enough, but is it too big?

Our goal here is to use scale factors to enlarge the rectangle representing the sheet until it encompasses the drawing.

11. Press ↵ to end the Scale command. Press Esc twice to remove the grips. Then Zoom to Extents. Finally, zoom to .75x.

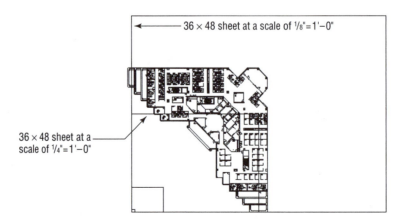

36 × 48 sheet at a scale of $\frac{1}{8}$"=1'−0"

36 × 48 sheet at a scale of $\frac{1}{4}$"=1'−0"

12. Erase the three smaller rectangles and move the largest one so the drawing is more or less centered in it. This shows that the scale of $\frac{1}{8}$" = 1'-0" will work fine for this drawing on this size sheet.

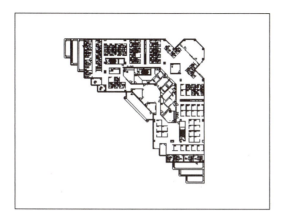

Getting Your Drawing Ready to Plot

There are several tasks required to prepare your drawing for printing. The extent of the necessary preparations will vary from drawing to drawing and from printing device to printing device, so this introduction to printing cannot cover all the tasks that you may need to perform. Instead, this section outlines the basic procedures for getting your drawing ready to print and refers you to other sources for more in-depth information on other plotting issues that you may need to address.

We will set up a plot for the same drawing—db_samp.dwg—that we used in the previous section, where we determined that, for this drawing to be printed on a 36×48 sheet, the best scale would be $1/8" = 1'\text{-}0"$. If you made a rectangle around the drawing in the last section, keep that there. We'll use it. If you didn't, that's OK, too. In the example we print to a file rather than a physical device, so even if you don't have a plotter that will handle the size sheet we are using, you can still try out the basic setup procedures.

Using the Plot Dialog Box

The Plot dialog box is where you make almost all the necessary adjustments to set up a plot. We will demonstrate a straightforward way to work your way through the basic settings to get a drawing printed. Specifically, we'll set a plotting

In this discussion, we use the terms "print" and "plot" interchangeably, as AutoCAD itself does. They used to have distinctive meanings, but they no longer do.

In this discussion, we are assuming that paper sizes, like 36×48, are in inches.

231

device, the paper size and orientation, the portion of the drawing to plot, and finally the location of the plot on the sheet.

1. Click the Plot button on the Standard toolbar.

2. The Fast Track to Plotting Help dialog box may come up. If it does, click the No button to close it. If it doesn't come up, move on to the next step.

Tip

Because so much has changed about plotting in AutoCAD 2000, the program offers a set of tutorials and demonstrations to help users of previous versions get familiar with the new procedures. If you are using a freshly installed version of AutoCAD, a dialog box appears when you click the Plot button. It asks if you would like to review the Fast Track to Plotting Help before you continue with plotting. If this dialog box does not appear, another user may have shut it off. If so, you can still access the Plotting Help by clicking Help ➤ Fast Track to Plotting.

3. In the Plot dialog box, be sure the Plot Device tab is active.

4. In the Plot Configuration area, if you already have a plotting device selected that will print 36" wide sheets, you are all set. Otherwise, click the Name drop-down list to open it.

5. Select the DWF ePlot.pc3 device.

The DWF 3Plot.pc3 is actually a device for putting a plot on a Web page, but it will serve our purposes in this exercise. If you have a printer that prints large sheets, you can select it instead.

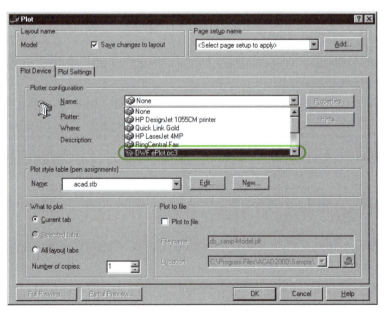

6. Click the Plot Settings tab to make it active. Notice that DWF ePlot.pc3 is displayed as the Plot Device in the Paper Size and Paper Units area. Click the Paper Size drop-down list to open it, scroll up the list, and select ARCH E (36.00 × 48.00 Inches).

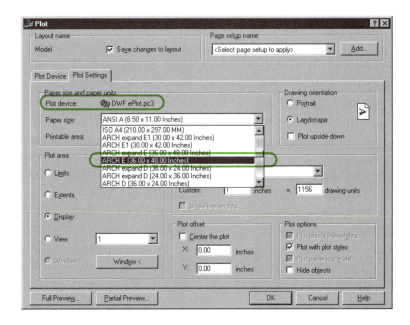

The options currently listed in the Paper Size drop-down list depend on which plotting device has been selected in the Plot Device tab of the Plot dialog box.

7. Be sure that Landscape is selected in the Drawing Orientation area. In the Plot Scale area, open the Scale drop-down list, scroll down, and select ⅛" = 1'-0". In the Plot Area section, click the Window button.

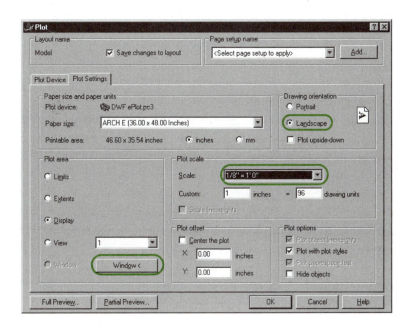

Landscape orientation turns the printed sheet so that the longer dimension is horizontal. Portrait orientation makes the longer dimension vertical.

233

The Window option is the most flexible of the five possible methods for specifying the area to plot. The others are more specialized and are not covered in this book.

The X and Y text boxes in the Plot Offset area allow you to fine-tune the positioning of the print on the sheet by moving it incrementally in the horizontal and vertical directions.

If you've already plotted your drawing a few times, the Partial Preview is a quick way to check that everything is correct before you plot. The Full Preview takes more time to generate and is better for the first time you plot a drawing.

8. Back in the drawing, if you still have the rectangle around the drawing, make a window around the drawing that just fits inside the rectangle. If you don't have the rectangle, make a window that just fits around the drawing.

9. In the Plot Offset area, check the Center the Plot check box. This will tell AutoCAD to automatically center the area to be printed on the sheet size you have chosen.

Now that we've gone through the basic procedure for setting up a plot, our next step is to preview the plot. Here is a look at the preview features.

Previewing a Plot

AutoCAD offers two kinds of preview tools—Partial Preview and Full Preview—both of which you'll find at the bottom of the Plot dialog box. We'll take a look at each of them.

1. Assuming that you have completed the setup procedure in the previous section, click the Partial Preview button near the lower-left corner of the Plot dialog box. In the Partial Plot Preview dialog box, you have an abstract diagram in the top half that displays a blue rectangle as the drawing on top of a white rectangle that's the sheet. Any problems that may occur in the plot are described in the Warnings text box.

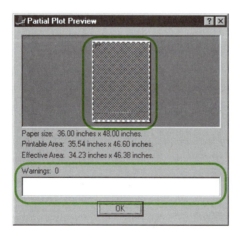

2. Click OK to close the dialog box. Then, back in the Plot dialog box, click the Full Preview button. The computer is busy for a moment. Then the entire drawing is displayed on a sheet of paper, very much as it will look when printed.

3. Right-click, and then select Exit on the menu to return to the Plot dialog box.

4. If you have an actual plotter ready to plot, you can click OK to plot your drawing. Otherwise, click Cancel to end the exercise.

Other Features of Plotting

The above exercise illustrates a quick and easy way of plotting your drawing, and it serves as a quick tour of some of plotting's setup procedures. Here are a few other features that are important in plotting but are beyond the scope of this book.

Configuring a plotting device: It is best to set up new plotters as Windows plotters and then take advantage of AutoCAD's System Printer option. The documentation for your plotting device is the best source of information about configuring that device. To learn more about the System Printer option, click Help ➢ Fast Track to Plotting and then, in the Plotting with AutoCAD dialog box, click on "How do I configure a plotter or printer in AutoCAD 2000?" Read the information on this page, then click on "Configuring a Windows System Printer." Read the information on that page and then click on the green text that says "Understanding System and Nonsystem Printers."

Controlling lineweights: Sometimes lineweights that look perfect on the computer screen turn out to be too fine to print properly. You can control the lineweight property using tools you've already worked with in earlier chapters. Lineweights can be assigned to layers in the Layer Properties Manager, or to individual AutoCAD objects with the Properties window.

Using plot styles: Plot styles control the appearance of objects as they are plotted. By using plot styles and assigning them to a drawing, you can plot the objects in a drawing with different properties—such as lineweight and color—for each plot. These Plot Styles can be saved separately from a drawing and assigned to several drawings. For more information on Plot Styles, click Help ➢ Fast Track to Plotting and then, in the Plotting with AutoCAD dialog box, choose "How do I specify pen assignments in AutoCAD 2000?" After reading the information presented there, choose any of the topics listed that have to do with Plot Styles and Plot Style Tables.

Where Do You Go from Here?

Plotting a drawing is an essential part of using AutoCAD. The plotting tools are powerful and complex. Getting comfortable with them will take an investment of your time. In most offices, the plotting devices are set up and maintained by a CAD manager or other employee with some expertise in using this equipment. Often, there are standardized procedures for using the system that is in place. When you are starting out, get help from these people and those around you who have learned how plots are made in the office. Try the Help tools on plotting that come with AutoCAD. They are extensive. For further reading on the subject of plotting, my other book *AutoCAD 2000: No Experience Required* (1999 Sybex), provides introductory chapters on Layouts and Plotting, while *Mastering AutoCAD 2000*, by George Omura, (1999 Sybex) offers a comprehensive look at AutoCAD's plotting tools and features.

This chapter completes *AutoCAD 2000 Visual JumpStart*. I hope you have found it to be a useful guide for beginning your adventure of learning AutoCAD. As you work with AutoCAD, keep this book near your workstation and refer to it when you have a question. I think you will find it useful as a reference as you gain some experience in CAD.

Glossary

Angle of rotation

The extent that objects rotate around the center of rotation, in degrees.

Annotation

Notes or other forms of readable information used in a drawing.

Array

An orderly pattern of objects. For the grid, the pattern is made up of rows and columns of dots.

Axes

The vertical and horizontal base lines for an *x,y* coordinate system.

Axis

A line about which a figure is symmetrical.

Base point

The point from which an action or movement begins. In scaling, the base point's location remains fixed while objects move toward or away from that point. In dimensioning, it is the point from which a group of baseline dimensions are all started.

Block

A collection of objects that have been grouped together and named, and now behave as if they were one object.

Block definition

The information about a block that is saved with the drawing and used to insert the block into the drawing. This information is the block's name, its insertion point location, and the geometric description of the objects that make up the block. This information is saved in the drawing even though you may not see the actual block on the screen.

Block reference

A representation of a block definition that is visible in the drawing. It is placed in the drawing with the Insert command.

Boundary edge

With the Extend command, a line that selected lines extend to.

Cascading menu

A sub-menu that flies out from a pull-down menu when an item on it is clicked.

Center of rotation

The point that selected lines rotate around. The center of rotation can be on one of the selected items but does not have to be.

Close

An option of the Line command that instructs AutoCAD to draw a line from the second point of the final line segment to the start point of the first segment, thereby closing the shape.

Command

A contained action taken by Auto-CAD, such as making a circle or erasing a line.

Command prompt

Text that says Command: on the bottom line of the Command window. It tells you that no commands are currently running, and it's waiting for you to start the next command.

Context-sensitive help

A process in the Help feature whereby information about a command is displayed while that command is running.

Controlling rectangle

In mtext, a rectangle that encompasses the mtext. It is created by the user at the beginning of the Mtext command, and its width is the line width for the mtext. Its height will change depending on how much text is used.

Coordinate system

A geometric set of rules for laying out points in an area or space.

Crosshair cursor

A form of the cursor that consists of intersecting vertical and horizontal lines. Their intersection is the current location of the cursor.

Crossing selection window

The selection tool that creates a window and selects everything inside it and everything that crosses the four lines that make up the window's dashed boundary. On the prompt line that displays all the selection options, it's called "Crossing."

Current dimension style

The dimension style that controls how new dimensions appear in a drawing.

Current layer

The active layer. All lines that are drawn while a layer is current will be on that layer.

Current text style

The text style that is active in your drawing. New text put into a drawing is made in the current style.

Cutting edge

In the Trim command, a line that defines where selected lines will be cut.

Default option

The command-line option that Auto-CAD will use unless you pick a different option. It's usually in angle brackets <>.

Default setting

The preset value that will be used unless a setting has been changed (customized).

Dimension line

The line that extends between the arrowheads and shows the direction in which the dimension has been measured.

Docked toolbar

A toolbar whose location has been temporarily fixed outside the drawing area, but near its edge.

Drawing area

The large, blank portion of the Auto-CAD screen where you create your drawing.

Drawing extents

A rectangle that is just large enough to contain all visible items in the current drawing. The drawing extents rectangle will change in size and shape as lines are added or deleted at the outer edges of the drawing.

Dynamically

Performed in such a way that the changes appear on the screen as you are making them (in "real time"), rather than after you have finished a command.

Extension lines

The lines that extend from the dimensioned object to the dimension line. They are usually perpendicular to the dimension line.

Font

A collection of letters, characters, and punctuation marks that share common features of design and appearance.

Ghosting

The effect seen when a line changes into dashes and dots to indicate that it's been selected.

Graphical User Interface (GUI)

The elements of the screen—such as the drawing area, toolbars, menus, and so on—that you use in working with AutoCAD.

Grips

Small squares that appear on strategic points of lines and other items. They are used to quickly modify lines in a set number of ways.

Hard copy

The printed sheet of paper, as opposed to the electronic file that is displayed on the monitor.

Implied windowing

A process by which a selection window is started by picking a point in a blank portion of the drawing area, when the Select Objects prompt is active or when no commands are running.

Insertion parameters

The three settings for defining the location (Insertion Point), size (Scale), and orientation (Rotation) of a block reference.

Insertion point

A point on or near a block that helps you place the block precisely in your drawing. You specify this point when you create a block.

Layers

Divisions in a drawing that act like transparent drafting sheets that are laid on top of each other. Some lines are on one sheet, and others are on other sheets. When you look through all of them, you see your entire drawing.

Leader

An arrow or dot with a line that connects text information about an object to that object.

Linetype

A style of line, such as dashed, dash-dot, continuous, center, etc. AutoCAD comes with 45 linetypes.

Magnification

The size of a drawing in the drawing area. Changing the magnification does not change the size of lines or other items in the drawing, just your view of them.

Mirror line

The line that serves as an axis, around which selected lines are flipped to create a mirrored image.

Objects

The lines, arcs, circles, text, and all other visible items in an AutoCAD drawing. Each type of object has unique properties as well as those in common with all objects, and is created by an individual command, such as the Line command for lines, and the Circle command for circles.

Offset

To create a copy of a selected item at a preset, perpendicular distance from the original.

Ortho

A mode that forces lines to be drawn horizontally or vertically.

Panning

The process of sliding the current drawing around on the drawing area without changing the magnification of the view.

Parameter

An independent variable in AutoCAD whose value usually has a default setting that can be changed by the user.

Pick

To place the pickbox on a line or other object and left-click to select it.

Pickbox

The form of the cursor that looks like a small square.

Pointer arrow

The form the AutoCAD cursor takes when it is not in the drawing area.

Precision

The accuracy with which a number is displayed. In AutoCAD units, precision is set for the display of linear and angular measurement.

Prompt

The information or choices on the Command line.

Properties

Characteristics of lines or of layers that have lines on them. Color is a property that can be assigned to a line or a layer. When assigned to a layer, all lines on that layer have that assigned property.

Pull-down menu

A set of commands displayed when the menu name is clicked.

Quadrant point

Any of four points at the top, bottom, left, and right extremities of a circle or arc.

Radius

The distance from the center point of an arc or circle to the arc or circle.

Regular polygon

Any closed shape made up of three or more straight sides of equal length. Triangles, squares, pentagons, hexagons and octagons are all regular polygons.

Regular selection window

The selection tool that creates a window and selects everything inside it. On the prompt line that displays all the selection options, it's called simply "Window."

Remove process

A technique for selecting objects that have already been selected, to remove them from the selection set.

Rubber banding

The appearance of a line stretching from the last point picked to the crosshair.

Running

Active and ready to be used without being selected.

Scale factor

With the Scale command, a number that controls how much an object grows or shrinks. In printing, a number that is associated with a scale and describes the magnitude of change of size from the scaled size to actual size. An object in $1/4" = 1'-0"$ scale would be 48 times larger at actual size. So 48 is the scale factor for the $1/4" = 1'-0"$ scale.

Scrollbar

A strip with arrow buttons and a slider on the side of the drawing. It is used for sliding the current drawing around on the screen.

Selection process

Any procedure that you may use for selecting a group of objects in a drawing so that they may be erased, moved, or otherwise modified.

Selection set

The group of one or more lines or other objects that have been selected through a selection process.

Sheet

A trade term for a sheet of paper. Paper used for plotting is often called a sheet.

Shortcut menu

A small menu that appears on the screen near the cursor when you right-click the mouse. It is context-sensitive; i.e., its commands will change according to what you're doing at the moment. It is also called a context menu.

Snapping

A procedure for drawing with the Snap tool. Lines are all drawn to lengths that are multiples of the Snap spacing.

Spline

Any curve that is defined by a set of control points, the placement of which will allow you to manipulate the shape of the curve.

Symbol

A picture or diagram that represents something else. In AutoCAD, symbols are usually made into blocks, but the two words are used interchangeably.

Tangent

To be in line with. With splines, a rubber-banding line becomes tangent to the last or first part of a spline curve.

Template drawing

A drawing used as a pattern for new drawings.

Text justification point

A point associated with a line of single-line text that is used to locate that text in the drawing. Each line of text has 12 possible justification points.

Text properties

The various characteristics that define the appearance of text, such as height, font, width factor, etc. The text style settings define the text properties.

Text style

A named group of settings that control the appearance of text in your drawing.

Toolbar

A grouping of icons, or small pictures, that represent related commands.

Toolbar flyouts

Sub-toolbars that are accessed from a button on the regular toolbars.

ToolTip

The small text box that appears on the screen to help you identify toolbar and dialog box buttons.

243

Tracking

A process of specifying the location of points relative to the location of other points in the drawing.

Tracking line

A temporary guideline that extends from a point and displays an option for the next line's direction. The crosshair with its rubber-banding line can be aligned with the tracking line.

Tracking points

Locations in your drawing that are temporarily used as the base of a guideline (tracking line). They are indicated by a small cross icon, which appears when the crosshair is momentarily rested at the location.

Tracking ToolTip

The small text box that appears on the screen to help you identify the tracking line and its characteristics.

Transparently

Performed while another command is currently in progress without causing the current command to be canceled. When commands are run transparently, they temporarily interrupt the current command.

Unit of measurement

The kind of quantity used for a distance, such as inch, foot, mile, meter, etc.

Vertex

The point where two line segments meet. For angles, the vertex is the place where the two lines that form the angle meet, or would meet.

View

The part of your drawing that is currently visible in the drawing area. It may be the whole drawing or an enlarged portion of it.

Wizard

Short routines that lead you through a series of steps to accomplish a task.

Word-wrap

A feature of most word-processing programs in which words are automatically placed on the next line below when a line exceeds a set length.

x and *y* axes

The two directions—left/right and up/down—that define the plane used to draw on in AutoCAD.

x, y coordinate

Two numerical values that designate, respectively, the horizontal (*x*) and vertical (*y*) location of a point on a flat surface.

x, y, z coordinate

Three numbers, separated by commas, that specify the location of a point in 3D space. The *z* axis represents the dimension of depth.

Zoom in

To increase the magnification of a drawing so that items in the drawing appear bigger, and the drawing seems to be closer.

Zoom out

To decrease the magnification of a drawing so that items in the drawing appear smaller, and the drawing seems to be further away.

Zoom option

Any of several possible ways to change the magnification of the drawing in the drawing area. Zoom options are all part of the Zoom command.

Index

Note to Reader: In this index, **boldfaced** page numbers refer to primary discussions of the topic; *italics* page numbers refer to figures.

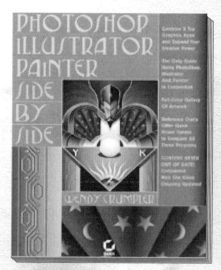

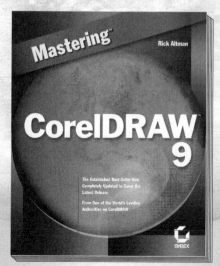
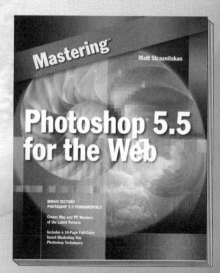

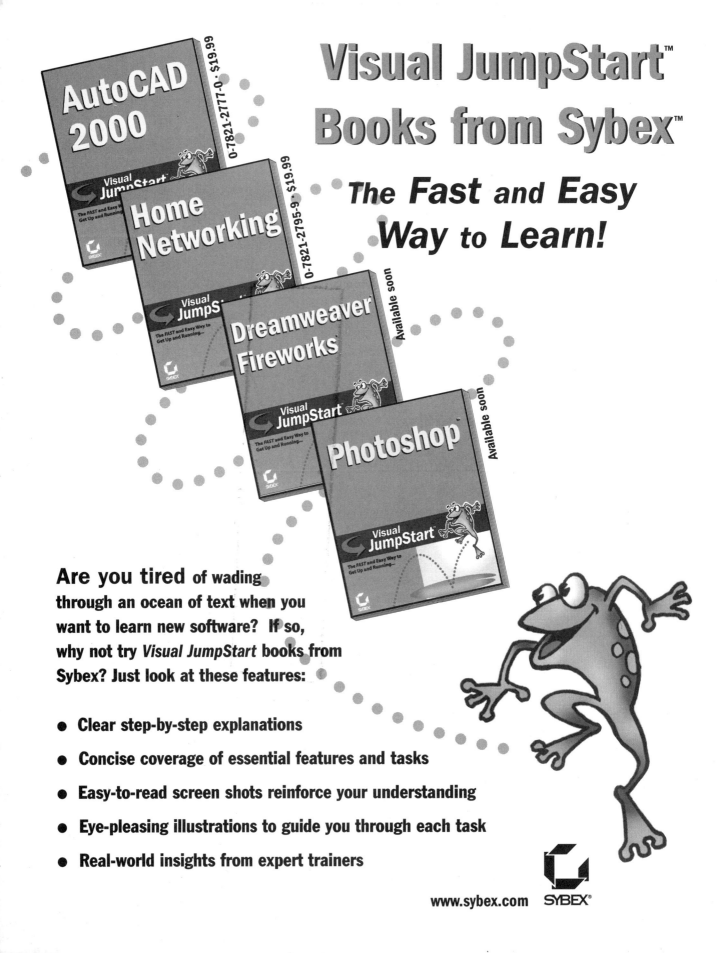